REPRODUCTIVE POLITICS

WHAT EVERYONE NEEDS TO KNOW

REPRODUCTIVE POLITICS

WHAT EVERYONE NEEDS TO KNOW

RICKIE SOLINGER

OXFORD
UNIVERSITY PRESS

OXFORD

UNIVERSITY PRESS

Oxford University Press is a department of the University of Oxford.
It furthers the University's objective of excellence in research, scholarship,
and education by publishing worldwide.

Oxford   New York
Auckland   Cape Town   Dar es Salaam   Hong Kong   Karachi
Kuala Lumpur   Madrid   Melbourne   Mexico City   Nairobi
New Delhi   Shanghai   Taipei   Toronto

With offices in
Argentina   Austria   Brazil   Chile   Czech Republic   France   Greece
Guatemala   Hungary   Italy   Japan   Poland   Portugal   Singapore
South Korea   Switzerland   Thailand   Turkey   Ukraine   Vietnam

Oxford is a registered trademark of Oxford University Press
in the UK and certain other countries.

Published in the United States of America by
Oxford University Press
198 Madison Avenue, New York, NY 10016

© Oxford University Press 2013

Library of Congress Cataloging-in-Publication Data
Solinger, Rickie, 1947–
Reproductive politics : what everyone needs to know / Rickie Solinger.
p. cm.
ISBN 978-0-19-981141-0 (pbk) — ISBN 978-0-19-981140-3 (cloth)
1. Reproductive rights—United States.   2. Contraception—Government
policy—United States.   3. Contraception—Law and legislation—United States.
4. Women's rights—United States.   I. Title.
HQ766.5.U5S673 2013
363.9'60973—dc23
2012029767

1 3 5 7 9 8 6 4 2
Printed in the United States of America
on acid-free paper

*to all those who work for the dignity and safety of pregnant
women everywhere*

CONTENTS

13 Contemporary Abortion III—Activism, Law, and Policy   80

14 Fetuses   88

PREFACE

Reproductive politics affects the lives of almost all of us. Rather than constituting private matters involving individual choices, nearly all aspects of sexuality and reproduction are matters of bitter public contention. In 2010 the fate of the entire federal health care reform project—passing legislation to ensure care for up to 51 million uninsured Americans—hinged on excluding abortion coverage. In 2011, state legislatures considered almost 1100 bills restricting or ending long-established reproductive services and passed a number of them. Meanwhile in the United States, according to the Guttmacher Institute, one out of every two women of childbearing age has experienced at least one unintended pregnancy, and low-income women are four times more likely to have this experience than middle-class women.[1] Sexually transmitted infections, some of which can lead to infertility, have been called a "hidden epidemic" affecting all of our communities, while funding for reproductive health services is uniquely threatened.

I was twenty-six when the *Roe v. Wade* decision legalized abortion in 1973, and like others of my generation assumed that it had settled the matter. Perhaps because I was relatively young then, perhaps because the political culture was less divided and divisive, perhaps because the claims of the women's rights movement seemed so persuasive, I didn't doubt that *Roe v. Wade* had established a new order, one that would change women's lives forever. The backlash against the civil rights movement was in plain sight in the early 1970s, for example, in the fight against affirmative action, the closing down of Great Society programs, and the growing political attacks on poor mothers who received welfare benefits. Yet many women's rights activists and others did not foresee the long decades of backlash against women's new sexual and reproductive freedoms that lay ahead. Nor did many white, middle-class proponents of these freedoms—in which I include myself—understand at the time what would be involved to ensure reproductive freedom for women across race and class lines. The forty years since *Roe v. Wade* have been an unending tutorial on the subject of reproductive politics.

In the 1970s, the Supreme Court's legalization of contraception for unmarried persons, along with its legalization of abortion, seemed to limit "reproductive politics" to mean pregnancy and childbearing. Soon, however, followed a number of revelations that expanded the parameters of this terrain. It was learned, for example, that for a period of years a number of physicians routinely sterilized poor women—often women of color—without their knowledge and their "informed consent." Producers of birth control pills were pressured to provide full information about the drug's range of potential side effects. "Informed consent" was and still remains at the center of reproductive politics, particularly as state legislatures debate what a woman must be told or to what images she should be exposed before being permitted an abortion.

Debates about public funding of reproductive health services, which began almost immediately after *Roe v. Wade*, have vastly expanded the range of "reproductive politics." These include disputes about the role of religion in civic life; about methods used to protest abortion; about what constitutes the family and its "values"; about the environment and what impact reproductive capacity and outcomes have upon it; and about the potential and dangers of science and technology.

In short, "reproductive politics" does not submit to simple mapping. No one can predict how current struggles over various aspects of it will be resolved—or even if they ever will. But in order to debate the issues productively, we need to know what they are and their full implications as they now stand. *Reproductive Politics: What Everyone Needs to Know* will step into this moment and attempt to bring the reader up to date.

As a historian, I believe it is critical to begin with a consideration of the past. For example, why was abortion legal for nearly a century in many states and not criminalized in all states until the second half of the nineteenth century? Why was Susan B. Anthony, one of the founders of the women's movement in the United States, opposed to abortion? In what ways do the legacies of slavery bear on the issue? And how were the lives of immigrants to America influenced by reproductive politics? Posing these questions reveals how deeply many of the issues we confront today are embedded in American history and invites us to consider how these issues have changed over time.

Throughout American history, laws, policies, and court decisions have given various governmental authorities power over aspects of female fertility and its consequences. These authorities have treated the reproductive capacities of different groups of women differently, in ways that have substantially shaped American society. Laws governing the fertility of enslaved Africans, for example, were crucial in facilitating the origins and maintenance of the slavery system. Laws and policies regulating aspects of female fertility have provided mechanisms for achieving immigration, eugenic, welfare, and adoption goals as well as supporting or hindering women's aspirations for first-class citizenship.

Many Americans have believed that the Supreme Court rulings that fully legalized contraception and largely legalized abortion resolved these issues in favor of women's "choice"— and have accepted these rulings. Other Americans have worked against these decisions for four decades and more. Legislators across the country debate, enact, or reject laws regarding the status and rights of the fetus; whether a pregnant woman who has used a controlled substance requires criminal prosecution or medical treatment; whether the state should limit, deny, or provide assistance to poor women who become mothers. Debates continue regarding whether "emergency contraception" amounts to abortion; whether state legislatures can mandate that an abortion-seeking woman obtain an ultrasound and a prescribed course of education before she is allowed the procedure; whether the new health insurance exchanges should include or exclude specific reproductive services; whether all babies born in the United States are US citizens; whether gay, lesbian, queer, and transgendered persons have the same rights to parenthood, variously achieved, as heterosexual persons; and whether the relationship between rules governing "gestational carriers" (surrogate mothers) and their clients are public business or private matters. Indeed, all kinds of questions about "choice" and about who gets to be a legitimate mother in the United States, who does not, and who decides—the stuff of reproductive politics—continue to resist resolution and to shape national politics.

With this book, I am aiming to equip the reader with material for evaluating these core debates, politics, and media coverage. Given the large number of topics that now clearly fall within the purview of reproductive politics, the process of gathering sources for this volume has been challenging. For the historical sections, I have relied on my own primary research, conducted over a period of twenty-five years, as well as on the books of my colleagues. To formulate and answer questions dealing with contemporary matters, I have relied on the research of sociologists, political scientists, and philosophers, and have turned to scholars of religion, the Constitution, immigration, science and technology, and other subjects. I have also drawn on recent studies—of such subjects as contemporary contraceptive use, and the age and distribution of abortion providers across the country—prepared by leading research centers. Materials from law-and-policy institutes have helped me track the current status of various legislative initiatives and legal actions.

I have been publishing essays, books, and edited volumes on various aspects of reproductive politics for a number of years. While my focus has principally been on the immediate post–World War II period, I have written about eighteenth- and nineteenth-century reproductive politics as well as on current debates. I am also a curator, organizing exhibitions, some of which involve the subjects of my books. These shows have traveled to scores of college and universities, where, I am pleased to say they have stimulated courses, symposia, and campus discussions.

I have always been committed to looking at the ways that laws and policies governing reproduction in the United States have valued the reproductive capacity of women differently, based on their race, class, ethnicity, and sexual orientation. As a historian I am especially interested in how these valuations have changed over time. For example, in the 1850s, owners of enslaved African women, eager to increase their human property, encouraged and even forced women to have as many children as possible. One hundred years later, state and federal public policies aimed to constrain the reproduction of African American women to reduce welfare payments, they argued, and to ameliorate urban problems. Laws and policies have changed over time regarding the value and the consequences of white women's reproduction, too. For example, in the mid-twentieth century, many unmarried white women who had "illegitimate" babies were expelled from school and pressed to put their babies up for adoption. Today, nearly one-third of white babies are born to unmarried women, almost all of whom raise these children. High schools, colleges, and even some employers accommodate single mothers who, along with their children, generally no longer suffer social stigmas. Throughout this volume, I return often to the subject of demographically driven reproductive privileges and punishments in the United States, a complicated arena to this day, but one that helps us, by its contrasts, to understand the distinctions and contradictions that reproductive politics embodies.

REPRODUCTIVE POLITICS

WHAT EVERYONE NEEDS TO KNOW

1

OVERVIEW

What do we mean by reproductive politics?

Beginning in the mid-1960s, women's rights advocates known as "Second Wave feminists" (a name inspired by nineteenth-century "First Wave" feminists who focused on winning the right to vote and other reforms) coined the term "reproductive politics" to describe their involvement in issues related to contraception, abortion, sterilization, adoption, and sexuality as well as other related subjects. The term has been useful because it captures the way politics lies at the center of these issues. For example, who has the power to make the decision about keeping or ending a pregnancy: the pregnant woman, a physician, or a member of Congress? Who has the power to define a *legitimate* mother, that is, a woman who has the right to raise her own child: a city welfare official, an adoption agency and its client, a judge, or the mother herself?

In the early 1970s, a number of court decisions, culminating in *Roe v. Wade* in 1973, granted women new rights, including the right to make decisions about their reproductive lives. Perhaps most controversially, these rights hinged upon a previously unknown or untried legal concept, the "right to privacy," roughly based on the "liberty" guarantee of the Fourteenth Amendment of the Constitution. Following these decisions, opponents and proponents of these new rights have used whatever means they can to enforce or erode them—from legislative to legal to populist, or taking their cause to the streets. Whatever the reaction to these new rights, the decisions have led to ongoing debate over whether women's reproductive capacities were public or private matters.

Are sex and reproduction private or public matters?

Many believe that a woman's decision to get pregnant, or not, and to have a baby, or not, remains a private matter, an orientation reflected in the commonly used term "choice." We may assess some choices as good ones, others as bad, but in the end, a majority of Americans currently believe that such choices belong to those most directly affected.

Others believe that reproductive capacities are public concerns and therefore subject to legislation. A number of recent laws and policies have had profound impacts on private reproductive decisions. For example, Congress's decision to deny federal funding for abortions and reproductive counseling services—the 1976 Hyde Amendment—has been perceived as mandating "forced motherhood" for those who don't have enough money to pay for private services. Together with regulations governing contemporary welfare provisions for low-income families, these policies reflect a belief that childbearing, and even sex itself, is not, or not simply, a private matter.

The public versus private debate has played out in a number of areas, such as in federal, state, and corporate policies governing issues like family leave, health insurance, and day care, which have constrained or expanded individual choice. Decisions about reproduction, including decisions about whether to get pregnant or not, to stay pregnant or not, to be the mother of the child one gives birth to or not—these are all shaped by laws and policies. "Personal" or otherwise, these decisions are shaped, too, by the various degrees of value that society assigns to the childbearing woman and her offspring, depending on such variables as race, class, marital, and citizenship status. These variables have varied over time. The impact of public policies and societal attitudes on the reproductive decisions of women may be a particularly difficult insight to bring into focus, in part because of the way that *personal choice* has become the dominant way of characterizing pregnancy and motherhood in recent times.

2

HISTORICAL QUESTIONS

When and why was abortion criminalized in the United States?

Since reproduction is a biological process, it is often perceived as timeless. But this process takes place within social contexts that shape and reshape its meaning, as ideas about sexuality, gender, race, class, and maternity change over time.

To begin with, for many decades after nationhood, abortion was legal in the various states and territories. A woman could legitimately ask a physician or a midwife to end her pregnancy, or "restore" her menstrual period, especially before "quickening," that is, before she felt fetal movement, an event only the woman could verify. Connecticut, with a large Catholic population, was the first state to criminalize abortion, in 1821. In 1857 the newly organized American Medical Association launched a campaign to make abortion at any stage of pregnancy a crime, and by 1910 every state had anti-abortion laws except Kentucky, where the courts declared abortion illegal. Arguments in favor of criminalization included the need to protect women from using poisonous abortifacients and from practitioners without medical credentials. Advocates of criminalization also stressed society's obligation to halt the declining birthrate among white Americans. And many stressed the need to protect the sanctity of motherhood and the chastity of white women; abortion, after all, supported the separation of sexual intercourse from reproduction. For many physicians and others, all of these concerns were generally more trenchant in the nineteenth century than the issue of fetal life. In any case, abortion was rarely prosecuted in states that had criminalized the procedure, especially before quickening.

Contrary to popular assumptions, no evidence exists for high rates of morbidity and mortality following abortion in the illegal era except in cases of self-induced abortion, a dangerous strategy typically used by the poorest women. In most localities, law enforcement officials generally did not arrest abortion practitioners unless they were accused of causing a death or unless pressed into action as part of an anti-crime crackdown. Illegal abortion remained very common across the criminal era, especially as ever-larger numbers of women entered the workforce and contraception was neither legal nor available. Some experts estimated that as many as 1 to 2 million abortions a year were performed in the United States in the decades before legalization. Today the number is about 1.2 million abortions per year.[1]

How did urbanization and "moral reform" movements in the nineteenth century shape reproductive politics?

During the same period that abortion was criminalized, largely during the urbanizing, post–Civil War decades, many young women lived and worked without the protection of their families and with newfound freedoms. In cities, physicians, midwives, pharmacists, and others made contraception and abortion available. In this context, moral crusaders organized to stamp out sexual license, often relying on religious justification and, at the same time, advocating that each state regulate sexual and family matters.

In 1873, a leading New York moral reformer named Anthony Comstock convinced Congress to pass a law placing the United States Post Office in charge of finding and censoring all "obscene" material—which came to include information about contraception and abortion—passing through the mail. Ironically, the law turned the mail service, previously a symbol of democracy (because it facilitated the free flow of ideas and information) into a vehicle for corruption and a site of surveillance. To protect the social fabric, Congress called on the Post Office to reaffirm its role as a filter. As a result, the system of dissemination of information and materials moved underground. Women who had the means continued to buy books and devices illegally. Those without money had little choice. In 1885, the cost of a diaphragm, for example, equaled a week's wages for a domestic servant or a factory worker.[2]

What impacts did immigration have on reproductive law and politics in the nineteenth and twentieth centuries?

This young domestic or factory worker was likely to be an immigrant in 1885, in a nation with the most demographically complex population in history. As immigration burgeoned at the end of the nineteenth century, Congress passed new laws governing immigration and naturalization, including legislation determining who would be allowed in, and once here, who could procreate with whom, and in the end who could become a US citizen. (Anti-miscegenation laws already outlawed procreation, cohabitation, and marriage between men and women of different races and provided severe punishment for violations.) For example, when Chinese men were encouraged to immigrate to build the transcontinental railroad, Chinese women were not allowed to join them, a policy that constituted an official effort to constrain the birth of Chinese or ethnically mixed American citizens. When the Chinese Exclusion Act of 1882 became law, less than 4 percent of the Chinese population in the United States was female; nearly sixty years later in 1940, the percentage had risen only to 30 percent.[3]

In 1924, the US Congress passed the Immigration Act (also known as the National Origins Act) in an effort to screen out "inferiors" and, as stated by the influential report of the

Sub-Committee on Selective Immigration of the Eugenics Committee of the United States of America, "furnish us the best material for American citizenship and for the future upbuilding of the American race." The act severely restricted the entry of Italians and other southern and eastern Europeans, reflecting which groups were deemed to reproduce worthy and valuable citizens and which were not. During the Great Depression, Mexican industrial and agricultural workers, long recruited to work in Midwest steel mills and the coal and crop fields of Michigan, California, and Texas, were now tagged as responsible for the Depression because Mexican women had "too many" children and the men took jobs from American workers. Mexicans were sent back to Mexico ("repatriated") in massive numbers, including many who had been born in the United States. Early twenty-first-century politics of immigration, especially debates about whether the American-born children of undocumented immigrants should continue to qualify as citizens under the Fourteenth Amendment, reflects a long history of debate about which racial, ethnic, and national groups should be allowed to produce and reproduce American citizens. This history also reflects centuries-old conflict about the "complexion" of America.

What were anti-miscegenation and eugenic laws?

Like immigration laws, US anti-miscegenation laws, prohibiting sexual relations between individuals of different races, and eugenic laws, designed to regulate sex and reproduction to ensure a "high quality" population, focused on certain groups as targets of public intervention for the "public good." For the century after emancipation, anti-miscegenation laws were enforced by whites in the American South who feared that mixed-race children exemplified the indeterminacy of "race," including the meaning of "white." Section 4189 of the Alabama Code, for example, read, "If any white person and any negro, or the descendant of any negro to the third generation inclusive...intermarry or live in adultery or fornicate with each other each of them must on conviction, be imprisoned in the penitentiary or sentenced to hard labor for the county for not less than two nor more than seven years." These laws were meant to keep the races separate and to protect the established meaning of "whiteness" in order to maintain the dominant system of racial control.

In the early decades of the twentieth century, eugenicists such as Madison Grant and Lothrop Stoddard became broadly influential, focusing on the project of reducing reproduction of those deemed "unfit." In essence, many eugenicists were interested in curbing the demographically and politically complex America that would emerge if reproduction proceeded without regulation. The field of eugenics generally defined the "unfit" as nonwhites, mixed-race persons, immigrants, and poor and working-class whites, as well as people with handicaps and criminal records. A pseudo-science that became popular during a period of heightened racism and nativism, eugenics justified targeting millions of women of childbearing age. In 1927, leading proponents Paul Popenoe and Roswell Johnson claimed that based on intelligence test results (a newly invented instrument at the time), as many as 10 million Americans (out of a total population of 120 million) were unfit for reproduction. At the same time, eugenicists argued that economically secure white women produced better babies, future adult citizens fit for sustaining a democratic nation.

In 1907, Indiana became the first state to pass a eugenic sterilization law; by the mid-1920s, twenty-three states had followed suit, and by 1940, nearly 40,000 eugenically motivated sterilizations had been performed.[4] Eventually, a number of these state laws were overturned, but not before the Supreme Court upheld the constitutionality of state sterilization laws and specifically approved the sterilization of one young, poor, physically healthy white woman, Carrie Buck, who became a national symbol of both the eugenics campaign against unfit reproduction and the nation's interest in racial betterment.

Carrie, the daughter of an indigent prostitute who the city authorities confined to an institution for the "feebleminded," was sent to live with the family of a policeman. As a teenager, Carrie, a good student, told her foster family that she had been raped and was pregnant. Her guardian immediately had the girl declared feebleminded and sent her to the same institution that housed her mother. After Carrie gave birth, the authorities declared that "the rules of heredity" dictated that Carrie should be sterilized. Justice Oliver Wendell Holmes issued one of the court's most infamous decisions when in 1927 he wrote for the majority in *Buck v. Bell*, "It is better for all the world, if instead of waiting to execute degenerate off-spring for crime, or to let them starve for their imbecility, society can prevent those who are manifestly unfit from continuing their kind.... Three generations of imbeciles is enough."

What access did women have in the past to voluntary sterilization?

Sterilization was not always a matter of coercion in the past. Women who wanted to end their childbearing and who had enough money to have a private physician might ask to be sterilized. In the first half of the twentieth century, a physician would generally agree to perform the procedure only if the woman met criteria recommended by the American College of Obstetricians and Gynecologists: the woman's age was multiplied by the number of children she had. If the result was 120 or higher and if two doctors and a psychiatrist also approved, the woman could be sterilized These criteria remained in place until 1970 when Second Wave feminists successfully pressed for women's right to decide these matters for themselves.

What do we know about women's reproductive decisions in the face of legal and medical constraints?

Clearly, until the last third of the twentieth century, most women had little control over their bodies or their fertility. At the beginning of the nineteenth century, the average number of children born to white women, was 7.07; as the population urbanized, more and more women attempted, via homemade and commercial preparations or abortion services, to limit their fertility, despite the growing number of states that criminalized these practices. By 1850, the white birthrate was 5.42 and the black birthrate was 7.90. At the end of the nineteenth century, the white rate had fallen to 3.87 and the black rate to 6.56. These figures are remarkable as, during this period of reproductive decline, contraception and abortion were generally illegal, inaccessible, or both. Women who attempted to control their fertility were in danger of being exposed and possibly punished by law enforcement. Millions took that dangerous step, which variously mixed desperation and resistance. Conversely, many poor women resisted cultural control over their sexual and reproductive lives by having babies. Sometimes these women suffered punishment as well, such as being sent to correctional facilities for "wanton and wayward" females, having their babies taken away from them, being denied public assistance, expelled from public housing, and sterilized against their wishes.

What was the process of legalizing contraception?

Contraception was gradually legalized during the Great Depression, when economic devastation required limiting reproduction. In the first decades of the twentieth century, crucial efforts supporting legalization were made by activist women, many of whom were feminist socialists, and by Margaret Sanger, the founder of the American Birth Control League in 1921—an organization that evolved over several decades and was renamed Planned Parenthood in 1942—and Mary Ware Dennett, co-founder of the National Birth Control League in 1915. Several early court decisions were key to legalization of contraception, including *Young Rubber Corporation v. C.I. Lee & Co., Inc.* (1930) and *United States v. One*

Package of Japanese Pessaries (1936) which together lifted federal bans on birth control and allowed many more women with private doctors to purchase contraceptive materials. In 1937, the American Medical Association cautiously endorsed birth control, but the Roosevelt administration would not touch the issue, fearful of being associated with the subject of sex and also unwilling to displease the Catholic Church. By 1940, with so many women in the labor force, over 70 percent of Americans approved of public health clinics dispensing contraceptives, and most states and cities no longer engaged in anti-contraceptive prosecutions.[5]

Five years after the birth control pill was marketed in 1960, the Supreme Court's ruling in *Griswold v. Connecticut*, citing a constitutionally protected "privacy right," struck down that state's Comstock Law, the last extant, against dispensing contraceptive information and materials to married couples. In 1972, the Court's *Baird v. Eisenstadt* decision validated the dispensation of contraceptives to unmarried couples.

How did "genocide" and sterilization abuse become matters of concern for women of color and their allies?

These Supreme Court decisions were handed down in the context of the emergence of a political culture favoring "reproductive choice" but also in the context of an emerging anti-welfare movement in the United States in which politicians and policy makers focused on strategies for reducing the childbearing of poor women. Tactics included state-mandated use and promotion of birth control and sterilization, policy targets that, together with other developments—including revelations about the infamous "Tuskeegee experiments," which left African American men with syphilis untreated as a way of studying the ravages of the disease—stoked the suspicions of many African Americans who came to believe that birth control campaigns amounted to "genocide."

Indeed, in the 1960s and 1970s, many women began to respond collectively to laws and policies governing their fertility, creating and joining with such organizations as Planned Parenthood, the National Welfare Rights Organization, the Committee to End Sterilization Abuse (CESA), the Committee for Abortion Rights and against Sterilization Abuse (CARASA), and many others. Women of color organizations often pulled strands from civil rights, welfare rights, and abortion rights movements to claim rights to reproductive dignity, including the right to motherhood, to reproductive health care, and to control over one's own fertility.

Coerced sterilization became a central focus of this work. While sterilization had become the most common form of contraception for American women by the 1970s, poor women, and particularly African American, Puerto Rican, and Mexican American women, often found themselves targeted by formal and informal public policies and widespread attitudes among hospital personnel supporting coerced post-delivery sterilization. Sometimes doctors and nurses obtained "permission" for the operation while the woman was in labor. After *Roe v. Wade*, the federal government paid for the sterilizations (100,000 to 150,000 a year) of poor women but not for their abortions.[6] Welfare officials told many poor women that only if they were sterilized could they keep their welfare benefits, and doctor-led sterilization campaigns emerged in major cities such as Los Angeles before the Department of Health, Education and Welfare issued guidelines in 1973 to prevent sterilization abuse.[7] In 1974, federal district court judge Gerhart Gesell tightened the rules mandating that "federally assisted family planning sterilizations are permissible only with the voluntary, knowing, and uncoerced consent of individuals competent to give such consent." Gesell also stipulated that the rules be written clearly and that a woman's decision to be sterilized or not would have no impact on her eligibility for welfare.

Even after these guidelines were issued, government studies found that, for example, the Indian Health Service and other providers of reproductive health services for indigent women of color were not adhering to the rules. Doctors in these facilities typically argued that they were providing the most effective birth control for poor women and reducing the welfare burden at the same time, a two-pronged argument that denied reproductive rights to poor women in the 1970s, even as these rights were defined and legally granted to other women.

What were hospital abortion boards?

Before the legalization of abortion, many women with private doctors appeared before "abortion boards," instituted in hospitals in the 1930s and 1940s and still functioning in many places into the 1960s. These boards were created for the purpose of hearing requests from women, often accompanied by their physicians, who petitioned a panel of psychiatrists, obstetricians, and other medical specialists for permission to terminate a pregnancy. Hospitals created standards for consent, and according to hospital reports, many institutions aimed to give permission to very few women, sometimes only if termination was accompanied by sterilization. In the 1950s and 1960s, a number of physicians whose essays about the work of these boards appeared in the *American Journal of Obstetrics and Gynecology* and other professional publications rarely addressed the issues of fetal life. Most typically, they wrote about the responsibility board members faced to protect and preserve the links between sexuality, femininity, marriage, and maternity. Most women who appeared before an abortion board were middle class and white, and they came with a statement of support from their personal physician. Still, many petitioners described the process of appearing before the board as having been frightening and humiliating, though in retrospect, one can observe that these venues did allow some women—for the first time—an opportunity, albeit constrained, to speak for themselves—before strangers and authorities—about their need and desire to make reproductive decisions.

What factors stimulated the push to legalize abortion?

As the women's rights movement established its agenda in the 1960s, many women began to organize and to speak publicly about reproductive rights, including abortion rights. At the same time, a rubella epidemic between 1962 and 1965 put many pregnant women at risk of giving birth to damaged babies; and a pregnant Arizona television personality, Sherri Finkbine, defied American legal and cultural constraints by traveling to Sweden, a country with more liberal access, in August 1962 to obtain an abortion after her doctor determined that she had inadvertently taken a medication containing Thalidomide, known to cause fetal damage.

These high-profile events had an effect on millions of working mothers, single women, women carrying damaged fetuses, emerging feminists, and others. In this era of vibrant rights claims, some feminist organizations typically associated abortion rights with individual autonomy, while others saw reproductive rights as protection against a history of reproductive exploitation and punishment, and focused on the right to be a mother as well as the right and the resources to access contraception and abortion.

Support for legal abortion was not limited to feminist organizations; it also came from groups opposing "overpopulation," proliferating welfare rolls, and government control of intimate matters. In the late 1960s, legislatures in Colorado, California, North Carolina, New York, Hawaii, and Washington reformed their states' abortion statutes. By 1971 over half of Americans favored legalization.[8] It was gradually becoming clear that outlawing abortion had failed. Illegal abortions were occurring in huge numbers nationwide, sometimes via organized groups such as the feminist Jane Collective in Chicago, which arranged hundreds of abortions a year.[9] All of these factors pushed medical, legal, and major political authorities to support formal legalization. *Roe v. Wade* (1973), the Supreme Court decision that invalidated all state laws outlawing abortion, was in part a pragmatic response to this entire complex of developments.

How many abortions were performed in the criminal era?

No one will ever know how many illegal abortions were performed in the pre-*Roe* era as almost all occurred in secret. Yet public health experts, law enforcement officials, physicians, and others who tracked abortion during the decades before and after *Roe* estimated that the number of legal abortions was close to the number of illegal procedures performed before *Roe*. Indeed, as far back as 1871, the *New York Times* reported that there were two hundred full-time abortionists in New York City. In 1890 doctors estimated that 2 million abortions were performed in the United States each year, and in 1921, a Stanford University study, using more reliable statistics than had formerly been available, found that one of every 1.7 to 2.3 pregnancies ended in abortion, and that about half of these were illegal. Other studies showed similarly high rates.[10] This is a surprising fact to many Americans who have believed that girls and women began to get abortions only in 1973, after the legalization of pregnancy termination. Equally surprising is the high rate of safe abortions in the late criminal era, when maternal mortality was more than five times more likely to result from childbirth than abortion.[11]

When did the anti-abortion movement emerge?

Despite the very large number of abortions that doctors and others performed every year in the pre-*Roe* era—many performed by easy-to-find illegal practitioners working in recognized locations—there was no organized anti-abortion movement in the United States until after 1973. In reaction to *Roe*, a growing number of people, identifying a pervasive "values crisis," called for laws and policies to restrain what they saw as an excess of equality. In their view, women were grabbing social power from men and challenging social stability in part by claiming reproductive rights, especially the right to have an abortion. Many who felt threatened by this crisis of values turned to religion for comfort and for answers, and as a vehicle for organizing resistance.

Immediately after *Roe v. Wade*, the National Conference of Catholic Bishops created the Pro-Life Legal Affairs Committee to work for the election of anti-abortion candidates, who were increasingly Republicans, and to work on a "pro-life" constitutional amendment.[12] The other center of religious and political work against legal abortion was the National Right to Life Committee, founded in 1974. In addition, by this time, fetal imaging was a routine practice. Being able to "see" and ascribe personhood to the fetus stimulated anti-abortion activism. After *Roe v. Wade*, state legislatures began to pass laws blocking public funding and mandating the consent of a third party (a husband, parent, or judge) for abortion. By 1977 most public and private hospitals did not permit abortions, which were now largely performed in free-standing clinics.[13]

What role did violence play in anti-abortion activism?

The anti-abortion movement quickly turned violent; the first clinic targeted by arsonists was in St. Paul, Minnesota, in 1977. Between 1977 and 1988, abortion providers reported 42 arson attacks, 37 attempted bomb and arson attacks, 216 bomb threats, 65 death threats, 162 incidents of hate mail, and 220 incidents of vandalism. The 1990s saw increased harassment of women and violence against health care providers, including the murders of physicians and other clinic personnel.[14] In 1997, an anti-abortion terrorist created "The Nuremberg Files," a website displaying names and pictures of abortion doctors along with personal information such as home addresses. The names of physicians who had already been murdered were crossed out. Abortion providers, describing the constant fear that the site caused them and their families, sued the creator of the website, Neal Horsley. A jury found the site "a true threat to kill," a decision that was later overturned by an appeals court.

How have US presidents dealt with the subject of abortion?

For two decades following *Roe v. Wade*, US presidents were either silent about the issue or actively opposed legalization. The *Roe v. Wade* decision was handed down during Richard Nixon's second term; however, Nixon made no public statements on this or other matters relating to abortion. Nor did President Gerald Ford. President Jimmy Carter was anti-abortion. President Ronald Reagan opposed abortion while in office and each year addressed the pro-life rally in Washington by telephone. President George H.W. Bush was anti-abortion. President Bill Clinton, who came to office twenty years after the legalization of abortion, was the first president to support abortion rights. He lifted the "gag rule" (a law prohibiting physicians and other employees of abortion-providing facilities from educating or counseling women about abortion) as soon as he took office and supported the Freedom of Access to Clinic Entrances (FACE) Act that prohibited the use of force, threats, or physical obstruction to interfere with a person trying to enter or leave an abortion clinic. Notably, during the Clinton administration, perpetrators of violence against clinics and personnel were most active and virulent.

Adhering to the prescriptions of contemporary party politics, George W. Bush was anti-abortion, reinstating the Reagan-era Mexico City policy also called the "global gag rule," targeting "partial-birth" abortion, and promoting adoption and abstinence, among other "pro-life" policies. Barack Obama rescinded the "global gag rule" and has generally supported reproductive rights.

3

FEMINISM AND
REPRODUCTIVE POLITICS

*Why is feminism so important to reproductive politics, and
vice versa, in the United States?*

Over the course of American history, questions about female
fertility have typically been dealt with in ways that eclipsed
the interests of women, individually and as members of various groups. Debates about who should have the power to
manage women's reproductive capacities have often been
linked to debates involving larger issues—social, cultural, and
economic, across the spectrum. Among slave-owners in the
antebellum South, for example, reproduction was primarily
an economic issue—owners desired to increase their holdings
in human property—as well as a concern about maintain-
ing traditional definitions of race and chastity. In the 1970s,
reproduction was tied in to the white backlash against the
gains of the civil rights movement and to issues about social
provision and urban poverty. Reproductive rights have been
associated with the desire of white people to maintain demographic superiority and the demand of environmentalists to
slow or halt population growth. To resolve each of these social
and political problems, various organizations and individuals
have proposed, enacted, and enforced rules governing wom-
en's sexuality and their reproductive capacities. Historically,
as we've seen, women themselves were generally excluded

from these rule-making processes. If anything, they were seen as the problem. When social problems persisted, women were immediately cited as the cause—for example, if large urban populations remained poor, politicians and others tended to look past such issues as low wages, scarce and expensive housing, inadequate day care, and lack of medical insurance and instead blamed women who made the "wrong" reproductive decisions, whether that meant having too few babies, too many, or something else.

Beginning in the mid-nineteenth century and continuing until the present day, feminists—those who claim that women have equal status with men—have worked to focus matters regarding reproductive rights, politics, and policy on the interests of women.

So-called First Wave feminists (c. 1848–1920) developed the concept of "voluntary motherhood," which, in part, asserted that a wife must have control over her sexual life and reproductive capacity. This early claim was the preamble to a number of other ideas and activities, supporting the position that women's health, safety, dignity, and access to full citizenship depended on their ability to control their own bodies and fertility. The content of the claim has changed over time; today most Second and Third Wave feminists, unlike First Wave feminists, support women's access to contraception and abortion. Over time, feminist activists have focused public discussion, law, and policy on the ways in which women's core interests depend on living in a society that grants them the right to manage their own bodies.

Why did Susan B. Anthony oppose abortion?

In the middle of the nineteenth century, as the country was rapidly urbanizing, abortion became more prevalent. Scores of full-time abortionists practiced in New York City, and medical and law enforcement authorities at the time estimated that a high percentage of pregnancies there and indeed nationwide ended in abortion. This development (as well as women's increasing use of contraception, particularly in the cities) deeply disturbed the first generation of feminists, women who met at Seneca Falls in 1848 and in a stirring Declaration of Sentiments proclaimed women's equality with men. Individually and as a group, they opposed the separation of sex and pregnancy and advocated "voluntary motherhood," a status that included education, the right to vote, and sexual control, that is, the right to say no to a husband's sexual demands.

However, they also disapproved of condoms, invented in the 1840s, believing that they would increase the opportunities for men to have sex outside of marriage. They disapproved of female contraceptives, too, the use of which, they believed, diminished women's claims to "moral motherhood." Contraception and abortion, argued these First Wave feminists, dangerously associated women with sexual pleasure, undermining the only dependable bases of a white woman's claim to social and familial respect—her physical purity and her moral authority.

Following the First Wave generation, how did feminist ideas about contraception develop?

In the mid-nineteenth century, First Wave white feminists declared that a woman's only dignified contraceptive strategy was exercising her ability to say no. In subsequent decades, a number of culture-changing developments doomed the Comstock Laws, which prevented dispensing contraceptive information and materials.

Again, urbanization was a key factor. The 1920 census showed that for the first time, more Americans lived in cities than in the countryside, a dramatic marker in a long process that took young women away from their families and into anonymous urban living and work settings. Between 1900 and 1940, female labor force participation rose 6 percent per decade. These wage-earning young women, rural trans-plants and immigrants, often completely unprotected by fam-ily, found themselves sexually vulnerable and facing a new degree of latitude regarding sexual decision making; they needed a means for controlling the consequences. The Great Depression of the 1930s further deepened all women's needs both to control their fertility and to earn money. World War II brought unprecedented numbers of women permanently into the workplace. By the 1950s, one-third of all women with children ages six to seventeen worked for pay. For African American women, the rate was higher than 50 percent.

Birth control advocates (including socialist feminists, notably Emma Goldman; a few outspoken physicians; and leaders Mary Ware Dennett and Margaret Sanger) recognized in the early twentieth century that women were desperate to control their fertility. They saw that women were educating themselves about their reproductive choices, through both reliable and unreliable means. As we've seen, women with resources could sometimes depend on the secret help of pri-vate physicians. Hundreds of thousands of women became willing to break the law to avoid having another baby. Indeed, while the Comstock Laws were largely in effect, between 1880 and 1940, white women's birthrate declined by more than half, and the rate of decline for African American women was even more dramatic.

Though both Dennett and Sanger argued that "birth con-trol," a term Sanger is usually credited with introducing in 1915, was a woman's right, they also variously linked contra-ception to eugenics. Reflecting common attitudes of the time, they asserted that fewer, "better" babies would improve "the race." In the first several decades of the twentieth century, both leaders pursued their work within a cultural context that continued to place special value on white "moral motherhood," a status that required "respectable" women to distance them-selves from explicit sexuality and from the separation of sex and reproduction. Consequently, many "respectable" women were afraid to engage in public discussion and public support for contraception. Ultimately, neither Dennett nor Sanger surmounted the persistent strain of racism that depended on establishing white women's purity by sexualizing women of color in contrast. Throughout the pre–World War II era, Sanger counted on the support of academics such as sociologist Edward A. Ross, geographer Ellsworth Huntington, and economist Thomas Nixon Carver; all were eugenicists.

In addition, an increasingly professionalized medical community began to seek control over all matters pertaining to pregnancy and childbearing; many physicians were not receptive to women-led or feminist efforts in this domain, from midwifery to lay efforts to disseminate birth control information. By the 1940s, Sanger's organization, now called Planned Parenthood Federation of America, to accentuate the importance of "planning" to achieve a strong nation and responsible individuals, began to cite economic self-sufficiency as a criterion for parenthood. Such emphasis on economic status served to heighten the sense that only well-off white women were entitled to regulate their bodies and reproductive decisions.

Despite these challenges, the work of Dennett, Sanger, and other feminists helped change attitudes surrounding contraception. During the Depression, responding to this feminist activism and to women's determination to control their fertility, a number of religious organizations, as well as the American Medical Association, reversed positions and endorsed the use of contraception. Greater numbers of medical schools began to train students in contraceptive practices. In a 1944 study of 3,381 physicians, Dr. Alan Guttmacher, professor of obstetrics at Johns Hopkins University, found that among physicians who had graduated from medical school in 1935 and later, 73 percent received training in contraception compared with only 10 percent of those who graduated before 1920.[1] These developments facilitated Sanger's fund-raising efforts to establish clinics for meeting the reproductive needs of poor women, including poor women of color. Labor unions, also imbued with a concept of "women's rights," became sites of information about contraception, as did clinics and other services organized by African American women's clubs committed to protecting the young women in their communities, to "advancing the race," and to making a claim for women's basic needs and the importance of reproductive planning to women's lives.

What was the reaction to the pill?

The birth control pill championed by Sanger and others was introduced to the US market in 1960. The pill is often linked to the "sexual revolution," a cultural development whose meanings sociologists, journalists, and historians are still debating. Most have described the sexual revolution as marking an era when sexuality was no longer considered primarily a vehicle for procreation. Rather, they argue, for both males and females, sexuality became a means of achieving individual satisfaction and self-expression. Scholars have debated many aspects of the sexual revolution, including when and where it started, whether the behavior ascribed to it amounted to a revolution, and whether it is possible to capture a general meaning of new sexual expressions without paying attention to its various impacts on different demographic groups. It is important to add that the sexual revolution—whatever it means—was happening during the civil rights movement. Some proponents and opponents of racial equality put reproductive politics at the center of their agendas. In the 1970s, some women of color such as Angela Davis argued that the mainstream women's movement was largely directed by whites who did not understand or address the concerns of black and Hispanic women. Subsequently the National Black Feminist Organization, the Combahee River Collective, the Committee to End Sterilization Abuse, the National Welfare Rights Organization, and the Committee for Abortion Rights and against Sterilization Abuse focused directly on reproductive issues. These organizations focused variously on promoting women's needs to control their fertility and not be victims of new and existing contraceptive methods. In particular, they opposed laws and policies that made contraception a duty rather than a choice, such as in the mandated use of contraception in exchange for favorable judicial or public-assistance decisions. These groups opposed the Hyde Amendment, which prohibited the expenditure of federal funds to pay for Medicaid funded abortion. They also opposed involuntary sterilization of poor women, a practice that continued in clinic and hospital settings for some years after women supposedly achieved reproductive freedom with *Roe v. Wade.*

In the 1960s and 1970s, some Black Nationalist men claimed that welfare departments and other public agencies encouraged (or coerced) women of color to use birth control, including the pill, as a form of genocide. The Nation of Islam and the Black Panthers, for example, asserted that contraception amounted to population control and that white authorities could deploy legal abortion to promote genocidal goals. Responding to the argument, some activist women turned the genocide debates into a forum for defining feminist, women-of-color reproductive politics and articulating the claim that reproductive rights include the right to be a mother.

How did feminist activists support reproductive rights in the 1960s and 1970s?

In the years around *Roe v. Wade,* the organized reproductive rights movement was dominated by the National Organization for Women, the National Abortions Rights Action League, Planned Parenthood, and other groups led mostly by white women, with mostly white members. The movement largely focused on laws and policies that would allow women to gain control over their sexuality and fertility as a strategy for achieving full citizenship; most often this meant concentrating on matters involving contraception and abortion. As we will see, the subsequent course of reproductive rights activism has had to deal with the fact that the early movement was racially divided and that white women and women of color often defined the core issues differently.

Before *Roe v. Wade*, the women's liberation movement used public "speak-outs," public hearings, and lawsuits as forms of public education, demonstrating women's determination in these forums and claiming their right to manage their fertility through abortion, when necessary. These forums also gave them an opportunity to draw on their own experiences to challenge the law and religious dicta. The willingness of women to speak in public before large audiences about such difficult and intimate issues was a sign of real change. Feminists spoke about and modeled the right of any female to tell her physician that she needed a prescription for birth control pills, becoming pioneers of patient-directed medical care. Near the end of the criminal era, feminists in Chicago, for example, organized highly successful, secret abortion counseling and referral networks and safe abortion services. These served as a model for groups in other parts of the country.

Before and after *Roe v. Wade*, reproductive rights organizations began to promote women's rights to safe, accessible contraception, using the law to gain rights for married and unmarried women, and to hold drug companies accountable for the safety of their products. These efforts were essential to the emergence of what has been called the "women's health movement." Barbara Seaman's book, *The Doctor's Case against the Pill*, first published in 1969 and *Our Bodies, Ourselves*, published by the Boston Women's Health Collective in 1971, were foundational texts for this movement. They helped establish an agenda, one that demanded public hearings on the safety of the pill, won product insert rules to ensure consumer education, applied informed consent rules to sterilization procedures, stimulated the establishment of legal centers to support reproductive rights, and turned many girls and women into feminists and women's health advocates.

4

THE LEGAL CONTEXT

Why are reproductive issues governed variously by
state laws, federal laws, and court decisions?

The United States Constitution created a governing system known as federalism, under which the states and the national government share powers. The Constitution is specific about which powers the federal government can exercise, reserving the remaining powers for the states. The United States Congress has the power to tax, collect, and allocate money to run the federal government. Therefore, among its other duties, Congress enacts rules and laws about how federal money can and cannot be spent. For example, Congress enacted the Helms Amendment in 1973 to forbid the use of foreign-aid funds to support abortion as a method of family planning. Congress can also pass laws that deal with crimes defined by the Constitution or those defined and/or punished by federal statutes. Thus, Congress has passed laws that protect abortion clinics against violations that constitute federal crimes.

State governments, meanwhile, deal with most criminal matters and matters having to do with family law, including marriage, divorce, adoption, child custody and support, and domestic-relations issues. Historically, before *Roe v. Wade*, all abortion legislation was crafted by state legislatures, and today many state legislatures are very actively involved in passing laws to severely limit or eliminate legal abortion.

A state court may hear a challenge to a state law that involves the interpretation of the state constitution, including, for example, a challenge to state laws regulating access to contraception or abortion. Federal courts, meanwhile, have jurisdiction over cases that involve the Constitution, the laws of the United States, and treaties made under the authority of the United States. In 2003, Congress passed and President George W. Bush signed the first federal law that banned a specific abortion procedure, the Partial Birth Abortion Ban Act of 2003. The Center for Reproductive Rights immediately challenged the bill in federal court and the judge blocked the enforcement of the federal law; ultimately the Supreme Court upheld the federal law in *Gonzales v. Carhart* 505 US 124 (2007).

The US Supreme Court hears cases brought by parties who are not satisfied with the decision of a US Circuit Court of Appeals. A state supreme court can petition the US Supreme Court to hear its appeal. Since 1973, the US Supreme Court has decided cases on whether there is a constitutional basis for determining the legal status of abortion (*Roe v. Wade*), the legality of contraception (*Griswold v. Connecticut*), and many other matters concerning reproductive experiences of women. But there were earlier cases that deeply affected these more famous decisions, such as *Skinner v. Oklahoma*, which was the first Supreme Court decision defining a reproductive right.

In *Skinner v. Oklahoma* (1942), a white man convicted of stealing chickens was sentenced to be sterilized under that state's Habitual Criminal Sterilization Act of 1935. Invalidating the punishment, the Supreme Court defined sterilization "as an encroachment on basic liberty." Justice William O. Douglas, writing for the majority, began to define a concept of reproductive rights, associating the right to procreate with "human rights" and with "the right to have offspring," implying that the right to reproduce is a basic civil right.

What did Roe v. Wade actually say?

By the late 1960s, a number of social and political developments had stimulated support for legalizing abortion. More married women than ever before were in the labor force and needed a full range of legal resources to prevent unexpected pregnancies and childbearing. Feminists and grassroots advocates of legalization, such as the Clergy Consultation Services on Abortion that provided abortion referrals, were building a large movement associating their goal with other "rights" claims of the era. The population control and anti-welfare movements argued that legal abortion would reduce social ills. A few state legislatures had liberalized abortion statues. And a substantial number of women all over the country continued to seek out abortion services wherever they could find them.

In this context, Sarah Weddington and Linda Coffee, Texas lawyers interested in challenging that state's anti-abortion law, filed suit in March 1970, on behalf of the named plaintiff, "Jane Roe," a pseudonym for Norma McCorvey, an unwillingly pregnant woman, and "all women similarly situated" whose constitutional rights were violated by state laws criminalizing abortion. The fifth circuit federal court found in favor of McCorvey's claim, writing that "the Texas abortion laws must be declared unconstitutional because they deprive single women and married couples of their right, secured by the Ninth Amendment, to choose whether to have children." The case was appealed to the Supreme Court, which heard *Roe v. Wade* in December 1971 and issued its 7–2 opinion on January 22, 1973. *Roe v. Wade* invalidated all state laws limiting women's access to abortions during the first trimester of pregnancy. State laws limiting such access during the second trimester were upheld only when the restrictions were for the purpose of protecting the health of the pregnant woman. In the majority were Harry Blackmun, who wrote the opinion, William J. Brennan, Chief Justice Warren Burger, William O. Douglas, Thurgood Marshall, Lewis Powell, and Potter Stewart. In dissent were William Rehnquist and Byron White.

The Court's majority based legalization of abortion on four constitutional principles: (1) women have a constitutional right to reproductive privacy and proposed governmental regulation of that right must be subject to "strict scrutiny," the most stringent level of judicial review used by US courts; (2) the government must remain neutral regarding a woman's decision of whether to have an abortion; (3) in the period before "viability" (the point at which the fetus is sufficiently developed to live outside of the woman's body), the government may restrict abortion only in the interests of protecting the woman's health; and (4) after "viability," the government may prohibit abortion, but laws must make exceptions that permit abortion when necessary to protect a woman's health or life. *Roe v. Wade* established a "trimester" concept of pregnancy: during the first third of pregnancy, women have an unimpeded right to abortion; during the following two trimesters, a schedule of increasing restrictions apply, based on women's health and fetal viability. *Roe v. Wade* associated the right to abortion with the privacy right named in *Griswold v. Connecticut.*

How did Congress respond to the Supreme Court's decision?

In part, Congress's response to *Roe v. Wade* was rooted in its ongoing attempts to blunt or overturn some of President Johnson's Great Society legislation. After *Roe*, some members of Congress focused on prohibiting Medicaid funding for abortion as the most effective available vehicle for curtailing access. But in the first years after *Roe,* most federal courts stymied these efforts, finding that it would be unconstitutional for a state to refuse to pay for a poor woman's elective abortion while agreeing to pay for other pregnancy-related medical treatment through its Medicaid program. The Bartlett Amendment of 1974, an early, unsuccessful congressional effort to restrict public funding of abortion, was condemned by the Congressional Research Service because, according to various court decisions, it would create illegitimate interference with the reproductive freedom that Roe guaranteed.

But soon, Medicaid funding for abortion did, in fact, become the chief battleground for reproductive politics at the federal level and also in the states. Liberal Republican senators such as Edward Brooke (R-MA), the only African American in the Senate, and Jacob Javits (R-NY) led the effort to allow low-income women, through Medicaid funding, the same access to abortion as other women. Representative Henry Hyde (R-IL) spoke for the anti-abortion side when he declared, "I certainly would like to prevent, if I could legally, anybody having an abortion, a rich woman, a middle-class woman, or a poor woman. Unfortunately, the only vehicle available is the HEW Medicaid bill." In 1977, Congress, with a number of new anti-abortion legislators in office, passed the Hyde Amendment (actually a "rider" attached each year to appropriation bills), forbidding the use of federal Medicaid funds for abortion.

In *Harris v. McRae* (1980), the Supreme Court upheld the constitutionality of the Hyde Amendment, with the court's majority agreeing that the federal government did not create a woman's poverty and therefore was not responsible for alleviating it. Justice Potter Stewart, writing the majority opinion, asserted that government did not owe a woman, even one with a medical condition incompatible with pregnancy, the funds for an abortion, though the government could not otherwise stand in the way of this woman's right to obtain a legal abortion. Stewart asserted, "although government may not place obstacles in the path of a woman's exercise of her freedom of choice, it need not remove those not of its own creation: indigency falls in the latter category."

The Hyde Amendment and *Harris v. McRae*, generally recognized as the first anti-abortion victories, had a major impact on the ability of some poor women to obtain abortions. In the late 1970s, the average cost of an abortion was $280, or $42 more than the average welfare check issued to support a whole family for a month.[1]

*How have subsequent judicial rulings and legislation altered
the rights created by* Roe v. Wade?

Over the past several decades, the Supreme Court has reviewed
many laws passed by state legislatures aiming to narrow or
even terminate women's access to abortion. Most often, but
not always, the Court has affirmed the right of states to enact
a wide variety of laws governing abortion, for example, by
establishing special regulations regarding minors' access to
abortion services; banning certain medically approved methods of performing abortions; and setting definitions regarding
the beginning of life. As of 2012, the Court's 1992 affirmation
of *Roe v. Wade* still stands. Following are brief descriptions of
some of the most important Supreme Court cases that have
reshaped *Roe*.

In *Bowen v. Kendrick (1988)* the Court found that the
Adolescent Family Life Act could grant federal funds to religious organizations that provide counseling services to adolescents without violating the First Amendment's establishment
clause. The Court decided here that even anti-abortion religious organizations could be trusted to offer education within
the context of a public school without furthering "religious
purposes."

In *Webster v. Reproductive Health Services* (1989) the Court
upheld the Missouri law stating that "human life begins at
conception" and placed restrictions on access to abortion. It
allowed the state to prohibit the use of state funds, facilities,
and employees if it chose to value childbirth over abortion,
and it allowed the state to test for fetal viability after twenty
weeks' gestation, although not to prohibit second trimester
abortions.

The Court ruled 5–4 in *Rust v. Sullivan* (1991) that since the
government had not discriminated on the basis of viewpoint
but had "merely chosen to fund one activity [childbirth] to the
exclusion of another [abortion], the 'gag rule' prohibiting physicians and other employees of abortion-providing facilities
from counseling pregnant women about abortion or engaging

in activities that encourage, promote, or advocate abortion as a method of family planning" did not violate the free-speech rights of doctors, their staffs, or their patients.

In *Planned Parenthood of Southeastern Pennsylvania v. Casey* (1992), the Court voted to "retain and reaffirm" women's right to abortion. It struck down the state's law requiring spousal notification prior to obtaining an abortion, ruling it prohibited by the Fourteenth Amendment's due process and equal protection clauses—because it placed an "undue burden" on married women seeking an abortion. The justices upheld parental consent, informed consent, and a twenty-four-hour waiting period as constitutionally valid regulations. This decision replaced the "strict scrutiny standard" with the "undue burden" standard for assessing obstacles in the way of a woman obtaining an abortion.

This change was significant because *Roe v. Wade* had argued that any law that placed a restriction on a woman's right to get an abortion before fetal viability would be subjected to "strict scrutiny," the highest level of judicial review that can be applied to a statute. As noted, *Roe* had defined abortion as a privacy right and placed it in the category of freedoms guaranteed by the Constitution; therefore, any restriction governing access had to be narrowly tailored and necessary to serve a compelling state interest. In *Planned Parenthood of Southeastern Pennsylvania v. Casey*, the Supreme Court ruled that laws that infringed on a woman's right to an abortion before fetal viability should now be tested by the less rigorous and more subjective "undue burden" standard, one that determines whether a restriction created a "substantial obstacle" in the way of a woman seeking an abortion. The new standard allowed state legislatures to enact mandatory waiting periods, "informed consent," parental consent laws, and other restrictions.

In *Stenberg v. Carhart*, (2000) the Court ruled that a Nebraska statute banning "partial birth" abortion was unconstitutional because the statute lacked the necessary exception for preserving the health of the woman; and because the definition of the targeted procedure was so broad as to prohibit abortions in the second trimester, thereby constituting an undue burden on women.

Gonzales v. Carhart (2007) upheld the Partial-Birth Abortion Ban Act of 2003, finding that the congressional ban did not impose an undue burden on the due process right of women to obtain an abortion. The *New England Journal of Medicine* identified the case as a landmark: "This is the first time the Court has ever held that physicians can be prohibited from using a medical procedure deemed necessary by the physician to benefit the patient's health."

5

RELIGION AND REPRODUCTION

What ideas have structured religious thinking about
reproductive policy?

Neither the Old nor the New Testament contains language specifically addressing contraception or abortion. Yet Judaism and Christianity—as well as other religions—have long taken positions on these matters based on interpretations of inspired texts. Regarding abortion, some religious interpretations have focused on whether the fetus is a full human being, and if so, at what stage of fetal development "ensoulment" or personhood is established; in other words, when does life begin? Two related key questions are, first, whether abortion is associated with either murder or with religious injunctions against the killing of innocent life—the Bible teaches, "Thou shalt not murder" and condemns killing the innocent; and second, how to weigh the value of the life or the health of the pregnant woman as against the value of fetal life.

Religious institutions also base ideas about abortion on questions about ecclesiastical authority; for example, does the individual have the latitude to make personal decisions about whether to end a pregnancy or does the teaching of the religious institution prevail in all cases? Further, do ecclesiastical interpretations take precedence over secular law in these matters, even requiring the adherent to be an advocate for religious principles in the public square?

How do various Protestant denominations approach abortion?

In the United States, Protestant moral reformers were the first to mount organized, public opposition to contraception and abortion, starting as early as the nineteenth century. Anthony Comstock and others worked tirelessly in the 1860s and '70s to rid the country of sexually explicit materials that appeared in public places, including circulars and newspaper advertisements for contraception and abortion. In 1873, the Young Men's Christian Association was successful in convincing Congress and state legislatures to criminalize these practices. Today some denominational organizations, such as the National Association of Evangelicals and the Southern Baptist Convention, continue their opposition to all forms of birth control, grounding it in the belief that all human life is a sacred gift from God. Opinions vary about the rare and dire conditions (usually associated with a pregnancy-induced threat to the woman's life) that may allow abortion.

A number of Protestant denominations, such as the American Baptist Churches, condemn abortion as a means of birth control and sex selection but teach that women who can approach the matter "prayerfully and conscientiously" might obtain abortions. Some denominations, including the Episcopal Church, the Evangelical Lutheran Church in America, and the United Methodist Church indicate that abortion is permissible only before "fetal viability" or under special circumstances, including those threatening to the woman's physical or mental health or in the case of "fetal abnormalities." A final group of Protestant churches, including Unitarian Universalist Association of Congregations and the United Church of Christ, supports "a woman's right to choose contraception and abortion as a legitimate expression of our constitutional rights."

What are the views of the Catholic Church regarding contraception and abortion, and how have they changed over time?

Some Catholic theologians have argued that over time the Catholic Church has seen abortion as a greater or lesser sin; others have argued that the Church has been consistent for centuries in asserting that life begins at conception and that abortion is the killing of innocent life.[1] In 1869, Bishop Spaulding of Baltimore affirmed the modern Vatican perspective on abortion, writing, "the murder of an infant before its birth is, in the sight of God and His Children, as great a crime as would be the killing of a child after birth.... No mother is allowed, under any circumstances, to permit the death of her unborn infant, not even for the sake of preserving her own life."[2]

In 1968, eight years after the birth control pill was made commercially available in the United States, many Catholics expected the Pope to moderate the Church's position against all "artificial contraception," that is, to weaken its opposition to the use of any method other than abstinence during a woman's fertile period. But instead, in *Humanae Vitae*, Pope Paul VI reaffirmed the Church's opposition to all forms of artificial contraception, sparking unprecedented and widespread expression of dissent among Catholic scholars and others, a response that has been called "the greatest uproar against a papal edict in the long history of the Roman Catholic Church."[3] Charles Curran, a prominent professor of moral philosophy, spearheaded the dissemination of a letter of objection signed by over 600 theologians and academics, and American bishops issued a pastoral letter in response, "Human Life in Our Day," arguing that dissent within the Church, in this case about contraception, can be legitimate.

Today some Catholic organizations, such as Catholics for Choice, continue to dissent against the Church's stance on reproductive rights. Members of these groups define themselves as conscience-driven and part of the "overwhelming majority of Catholics in the U.S. [who] support access to legal abortion, contraception, and comprehensive sexuality education as well as separation of church and state."[4] Indeed, sexually active heterosexual Catholic women over eighteen are as likely (98 percent) to have used some form of contraception banned by the Vatican as women in the general population (99 percent). In addition, a Guttmacher Institute study of 9,500 women showed that Catholic women have abortions at the same rate as other women.[5]

What does Islam teach about reproductive control?

The Muslim Quran specifically describes four stages of embryonic development, each lasting forty days. At the end of the third stage—120 days or three months after conception—the Quran teaches that the human spirit enters the body, and the fetus is considered "another creation," or human. The Prophet Muhammad and numerous imams have commented extensively on the Quran's account, generally affirming traditional injunctions against all abortion except to save maternal life. In recent years, however, some authorities have initiated new jurisprudential directions responsive to the Muslim interest in defining "the lesser of two evils" which might involve, for example, a ruling that permits abortion of a severely damaged fetus. Muslim authorities define their "respect for life" as discouraging all non-therapeutic abortions, although family planning is widely considered compatible with the religion's teachings.

Shiite authorities generally forbid abortion after implantation of a fertilized ovum. Ayatollah Khameneii wrote, "The shari'a does not permit the abortion of a fetus...there is no difference between a fetus less than or greater than the four months gestation with regard to this matter." The four Sunni schools of thought agree that abortion should not occur after four months' gestation except to save the life of the mother; there is disagreement among Sunni imams regarding the circumstances that permit abortion within the first three months.

There are fifty-seven members of the Organization of Islamic Conference. Most of these forbid abortion except when a woman's life is threatened, but twelve members, mostly former Soviet Socialist Republics, plus Turkey (which guaranteed the right to reproductive health in its 1982 constitution), Tunisia, and Bahrain (a politically and socially conservative Muslim state) permit widespread access to abortion.

A growing number of Muslim countries have begun to permit therapeutic abortion in cases of fetal anomaly, including Benin, Burkina Faso, Chad, Guinea, Kuwait, Qatar, and Iran. This shift is due to a number of factors, including the writings of some leading authorities within both Sunni and Shiite traditions allowing this practice under limited circumstances; the problems associated with ever-expanding populations; health care costs in the midst of numerous health crises and constrained budgets; the number of illegal abortions that occur each year; the information provided by diagnostic imaging; and the inability of poor families to adequately care for babies born with severe anomalies. In 2005, the Parliament of Iran passed a law allowing therapeutic abortions when a fetus less than four months of age, that is, before the spirit is breathed into it, is suffering from profound developmental delay or profound deformations or malformations that cause extreme suffering or hardship for the mother, including life endangerment, or for the fetus. The mother and the father must both consent to the procedure.[6]

How does Judaism regard abortion and contraception?

Judaism also has no singular ruling on these matters but expects every case to be considered on its own merits and a decision made after consultation with a rabbi. Jews today take a variety of stances, although most want to turn to their own traditions and conscience instead of being governed by civil authorities regarding abortion and contraception. Like members of other religious groups, they often base their opinion on the woman's reason for seeking termination. Many orthodox Jews would approve of or even insist upon abortion in cases where continuing the pregnancy would put the woman's life in danger. According to some, Jewish law is lenient about abortion during the first forty days of pregnancy, before the fetus has become a full person. Reform Jews tend to believe that any decision should be left up to the pregnant woman. Reform Judaism strongly supports the use of contraception and sex education to prevent unwanted pregnancy.

What impact have religious teachings had on women's reproductive practices in the United States today?

Most research has measured *attitudes*, not behavior, according to religious affiliation. But a major recent study of more than 1,500 women, age twenty-six and younger, who had made a decision as to whether to stay pregnant while unmarried showed that women who identified themselves as conservative Protestants (a term usually associated with fundamentalist denominations) were the least likely to report having had an abortion. The study found that, in general, young women often had a difficult time reconciling their decision with their religious training and beliefs, given other considerations, including financial, social, and health. Overall, the study found that a young woman's high school and college grades and her parents' level of education influenced her decision more strongly than did her religion. In fact, this first longitudinal study of these matters suggested that young women who had attended private religious schools were more likely to have abortions than those from public schools.[7] Other studies have found that among those obtaining abortions, nearly one-third report themselves as Catholic.

In 2011, the Pew Research Center reported that a small majority of Catholics (52 percent) say that abortion should be legal in all or most cases; 45 percent believe that in almost no circumstance should abortion be legal. Evangelical Protestants remain the religious group most opposed to legal abortion, with just 34 percent saying abortion should be legal and 64 percent saying it should be illegal in all or most cases.

How does the First Amendment's "establishment clause," guaranteeing religious freedom, affect matters?

Like Congress, many state legislatures are considering or enacting new restrictions on a woman's right to have an abortion. Those who support these restrictions generally cite religious objections to, for example, private health insurance plans covering abortion, or their belief that women should be compelled to view images of "the unborn child" before having an abortion. Some legal scholars claim that the new restrictions violate the First Amendment's "establishment clause," which guarantees the separation of church and state. They argue specifically that by imposing such restrictions, the government is allowing one group's religion primacy over the health care and reproductive lives of all women, many of whom have different beliefs from those embodied in the restrictions.

Opponents of this legislation also claim that the abortion restrictions discriminate on the basis of gender, since women primarily have to deal with the matter of pregnancy termination; legislators are not considering analogous restrictions on funding for Viagra or surgical procedures that terminate male fertility. Finally, some critics have argued that legislative restrictions violate other constitutional principles including the privacy right at the core of *Roe v. Wade,* and create demonstrable "undue burdens" for women seeking abortions.

6

POPULATION ISSUES AND REPRODUCTIVE POLITICS

What is the state of population growth in the United States today, and how is it affected by immigration?

According to the 2010 census, the US population has grown 9.7 percent (adding about 27 million people, including about 13 million immigrants) during the past decade, the slowest growth rate since the Great Depression. The birth rate, 13.5 births for every 1,000 people in 2009, is down from 14.3 in 2007; in 1909, the rate was 30. Despite these slower growth rates, the United States remains one of the fastest growing industrialized countries, accounting for 4.6 percent of the world's population and 33 percent of global consumption. Most environmentalists predict catastrophic depletion of natural resources and despoliation of the natural environment if the United States doesn't achieve negative population growth and curtail consumption soon. On the other hand, many economists discuss the challenges of an aging workforce, including the dramatic spike in Social Security outlays that will not be replenished by the contributions of a large enough cohort of younger workers if birth rates remain low. Some demographers point out that the immigrant population is the only sector reproducing itself sufficiently to boost the workforce, protect the future of Social Security, and generally create an age-balanced population.

In short, debates about whether the United States is facing a "population crisis" are ongoing and continue to shape initiatives concerning immigration policy today.[1]

Just as in the late-nineteenth and early twentieth century, immigration currently has a direct effect on reproductive politics. Immigration promotes a healthy birthrate, but some Americans express strong feelings about according partial or full citizenship rights to *illegal* immigrants. In 2011, nearly one in four Americans favored ending birthright citizenship, that is, supported changing the Constitution to bar citizenship for children born in the United States to undocumented parents.[2] Polls also show that after years of congressional inaction, and especially during times of economic stress, most Americans believe that the immigration system is broken. Arizona has led other states, passing popular legislation that makes the presence and hiring of undocumented persons in the state a crime. Concerns have focused on the changes in the makeup of the population: in 1970, 6 percent of the US population was Hispanic or Asian; today these groups equal 20 percent. Demographers predict that by 2050, the non-Hispanic white population will have fallen to 50 percent of the total population, with Hispanics and Asians accounting for one-third. Even more alarming to some whites is that while the 2010 census showed that the majority of children in the country were white in the year of the census, the Census Bureau reported that on July 1, 2011, "minorities," that is, anyone who is not a single-race non-Hispanic white, made up 50.4 percent of the nation's population younger than age one, a development that occurred sooner than demographers had expected.[3]

Many Americans oppose immigration because they believe that immigrants—and their many children—will take jobs from American citizens and depress wages, although economic studies have not conclusively affirmed or denied these claims. In addition, while immigrants pay property and sales taxes, and an estimated two-thirds of unauthorized immigrants pay Social Security and Medicare taxes—benefits they are generally unable to access in most states—their families can access tax-supported services such as K-12 schools and emergency medical care, contributing to the widespread perception that immigrant populations are straining municipal and state budgets, a belief based largely on the high birthrates of immigrant women. Some Americans tie their opposition to immigration specifically to the high Hispanic birthrate, even while the most recent information suggests that immigration from Mexico has plummeted.[4] Nevertheless, between 2000 and 2010, the Hispanic birthrate climbed by 14 percent, with concentrations in the West and South, while overall the US rate declined, especially in the Northeast and Midwest, a development that has significant implications for apportioning congressional representation.

What is the link between citizenship and reproductive politics?

The Fourteenth Amendment, passed in the aftermath of the Civil War and designed to affirm the citizenship status of formerly enslaved persons, conferred the rights of citizenship, including the guarantee of equal protection under the law, on everyone born in the United States. This is generally referred to as "birthright citizenship." In 1898, the Supreme Court reaffirmed the fundamental principle that children born on US soil are automatically citizens without regard to their parents' status; this principle has been settled law for more than a century.

Some state legislators have proposed requiring states to deny standard birth certificates to children born to undocumented immigrant parents as part of an effort to eliminate an alleged incentive for illegal immigration. Immigrant rights groups say that most immigrants come to the United States looking for work and to join their families, not to give birth. According to rights groups, since a high percentage of immigrants are of childbearing age and have children after they immigrate, removing birthright citizenship would simply create a larger pool of undocumented, stateless persons without solving the immigration problems the country faces. In addition, changes to the Constitution must occur via prescribed, nationwide processes and cannot be accomplished by singular state legislatures.

Reproductive rights advocates argue that, in part because of anti-immigrant and "population crisis" sentiments, the reproductive rights of immigrant women are often trammeled, on the one hand, by Medicaid rules that deny coverage to low-income women, including coverage for maternity services for those who have been US residents for fewer than five years, and on the other hand, by the Hyde Amendment. Also, even when reproductive and maternity services are available, immigrant women are too often unable to find linguistically and culturally compatible providers.[5]

7

PUBLIC POLICY AND REPRODUCTIVE POLITICS

How do policies such as day-care funding and family leave shape women's reproductive decisions?

Only about one in five US households has a male wage earner and a full-time female "homemaker." In fact, women are the primary earners in 40 percent of American households and head 85 percent of single-parent households.[1] Therefore, access to affordable day care has become a key factor in a woman's decision to reproduce. Unlike most industrialized countries, the United States does not have a national child-care policy and provides very limited subsidized care for young children (or dependent elders). In fact, lower-income families typically pay 32 percent of their income on day care, making reproduction unaffordable for many.

A recent study of twenty-one countries with "high-income economies" found that the United States ranks twentieth in providing parental leave, with only twenty-four weeks of combined protected job leave for a two-parent family. In addition, it is one of only two countries in this group that offers no paid parental leave.[2]

How have gender-based wage disparities intersected with reproductive politics?

American women who work full-time average 77 cents for every dollar a man earns. The disparity is even steeper when race and ethnicity are taken into account; for example, a Latina woman earns 52 cents for every dollar earned by a white non-Hispanic male. This means that the typical female worker makes about $10,000 a year less than the average male worker. Lower wages translate into lower unemployment benefits and major loss of income in retirement because of scantier savings and smaller pensions, thereby sustaining low income over time. Wage disparities, especially in combination with the lack of family leave benefits and child-care services, further compromise the ability of women to have children and support a family.[3]

How have policies regarding drugs influenced reproductive politics?

Recent research has shown that legal chemical substances—alcohol and tobacco—are potentially more harmful to fetuses and much more commonly used by pregnant women than cocaine and other illegal drugs. Nevertheless, in the context of the ongoing "war on drugs"—in a society that provides very few treatment centers willing to accept pregnant drug users—the criminal justice system, along with family and drug courts, brings cases against largely poor, pregnant drug users by arguing for "fetal rights." Consequently, many pregnant women have been detained, prosecuted, and incarcerated for harming their fetuses.[4] Certainly pregnant women should avoid exposing their fetuses to all harmful substances. But we now have better information about the effects of drugs on fetuses than earlier; for example, national longitudinal studies show that claims in the 1980s about the impact of maternal cocaine use on fetuses were exaggerated and incorrect, and yet legislators continue to structure law enforcement work targeting low-income women who use opiates, but not users of other harmful substances of whatever social class.[5]

Advocates for pregnant women argue that when courts focus on protecting the fetus and criminalizing the mother, they actually further endanger maternal and fetal health by discouraging a pregnant, drug-using woman's efforts to get proper treatment. Courts are in effect demanding that poor, addicted, pregnant women must provide their fetuses with health care, in the form of anti-drug therapy, even though this treatment is not available, and even if it were, these women could not afford to pay for it. Moreover, the focus on fetuses deflects political and policy attention from social crises such as this very lack of affordable medical care and the need for more programs to support pregnant and parenting women.

How does the current national welfare policy affect reproductive politics?

In 1935, during the Great Depression, Title IV of the Social Security Act created the Aid to Dependent Children program, the country's first federal effort to provide assistance for poor children. With various expansions and adjustments, this program, now known as "welfare," gave cash assistance to poor mothers and their children. ADC (later, Aid to Families with Dependent Children, or AFDC) was an entitlement program that guaranteed cash benefits to all recipients whose income and resources were below state-determined eligibility levels, subject to federal guidelines and limits. Between 1935 and 1995, benefits to poor mothers and their children waxed and waned depending on the political status of "anti-poverty" initiatives at any given time. Presidents Lyndon Johnson and Richard Nixon expanded welfare programs, for example, and President Ronald Reagan, in part by highlighting the number of African American recipients—in truth, always a minority of total recipients—and raising questions about the legitimacy of their claims to benefits, laid the political groundwork for terminating the AFDC program.[6]

In the mid-1990s, in an era of intensifying hostility toward public provision for the poor, President Bill Clinton famously directed Congress to "end welfare as we know it." Congress replaced AFDC with Temporary Assistance to Needy Families (TANF), a more restricted and restrictive non-entitlement form of support that gave the states enormous latitude to decide how to respond to poor families. Underscoring a new commitment to motherhood as an economic status, TANF guidelines say that no woman can receive benefits for herself and her minor children for more than five years during her life and that to receive benefits, a woman, including one who has recently given birth, must participate in a "work-activity" up to forty hours a week, more hours than any other group of new mothers works on average. Focusing eligibility on moral as well as economic grounds, the federal government, through TANF, expects states to develop programs that both discourage potential recipients from unmarried pregnancy and encourage marriage for recipients. Critics of these policies point out that poverty and new worldwide norms, not immorality, contribute to delayed marriage. Under TANF, states are spending less on cash assistance and more on education and training, child care, and other work supports to help families achieve self-sufficiency. This is a strategy designed for good economic times but one that leaves many unemployed heads of household without cash assistance during periods of high unemployment rates.

How does policy governing foster care and other child-protective services affect reproductive politics?

The foster care system exists to provide alternate care settings for children who are victims of neglect and abuse within their current residences. Children of all races are equally likely to require foster care, but a significantly higher percentage of African American children are placed within this system than children of other races and ethnicities. Also, according to recent studies, the foster care option is extremely expensive, involving law enforcement, health care, judicial, and foster care system responses. Taking a child away from his or her family has been shown to trigger short- and long-term direct economic effects and emotional consequences for the nearly 300,000 children entering the system each year and their mostly poor parents.[7]

Critics argue that while the foster care option can be useful and in some cases is necessary, the system is harmed by federal funding mandates, which, in the child welfare arena, too often require that children be sent into foster care even when, with proper services, the original family might be preserved. For example, states can use only about 10 percent of federal funds dedicated to child welfare for family services and supports to avoid child removal, based on local guidelines. Research shows that if more public funds were devoted to family support, family strengthening, and family reunification services, the number of poor families that were broken up would diminish as would all categories of costs.[8]

In addition, middle-class parents are far less likely to come to the attention of child welfare officials than poor parents, even when their parenting behavior is potentially as dangerous or more dangerous to the welfare of the child. Current research shows that state child welfare directors report that cultural misunderstandings and other bias-driven problems encourage staff to remove children from their low-income birth parents, raising the issue of common presumptions about economic qualifications for parenthood.

8

TEENAGE AND SINGLE PREGNANCY IN THE UNITED STATES

How have attitudes about single and teenage pregnancy changed since World War II?

Once again, as with so much of reproductive politics, the question immediately and urgently touches upon race and class. Between about 1945 and 1970, with many institutions still widely enforcing racial segregation, public policies and social service agencies developed racially separate programs for single women who became pregnant. Community authorities and parents prescriptively pressed unwed, pregnant, white females to leave their communities and spend the second half of their pregnancies in all-white maternity homes or elsewhere, give up their babies for adoption, and then return to the community, keeping the "illegitimate" episode a secret. This period marked the invention of the concept—and the functioning—of a national "adoption market," largely serving a white population.

At the same time, policy makers and others penalized unwed mothers of color—for example, by mandating the loss of welfare benefits and public housing, incarceration, and sterilization. Families of color did not generally favor adoption, preferring to acknowledge, keep, and raise their babies born "out of wedlock." Though responses to unwed pregnancy varied across races in these decades, most involved coercion, loss, and punishment for all groups of women.

In 2010, rates of teen pregnancy were at historic lows, 44 percent lower than the peak in 1991, and 64 percent lower than the all-time high levels in 1957 during the baby boom, when many girls married and had their first babies in their teens.[1] On the other hand, the rates of unwed childbearing are much higher than in the past, with more than 40 percent of all babies in the United States born to unmarried mothers. Demographically, 73 percent of non-Hispanic black children, 53 percent of Hispanic children, and 29 percent of non-Hispanic white children are born to unmarried women.[2] Many policy makers seem to ascribe this less to race than to poverty, arguing that single motherhood causes poverty while marriage reduces it.[3] Others argue that the causes of poverty are more complex; that marrying a poor man does not typically make a poor woman less poor; and that many poor women with few clear life options or opportunities are likely to choose motherhood as one of the only available routes to adulthood.[4] While having a baby outside of marriage may deepen poverty today, a mother (especially if she is not a teenager or black) is generally no longer the target of societal shame. The falling away of this stigma has been an important factor in dramatically reducing the number of babies that white unwed mothers give up for adoption.

It is worth noting that the increases in US rates of unmarried pregnancy and motherhood are occurring as part of worldwide trends in the same direction. For example, many Western European countries have higher rates of unwed childbearing than the United States, and all European countries show substantial rises in the past thirty years, with the Netherlands, Spain, and Ireland having the sharpest increases.

What rights do teenagers have regarding reproductive health care?

Following *Roe* and the association of reproductive rights with the right to privacy, states have expanded the rights of minors to consent to health care, including the right to obtain contraception. More than half the states, recognizing that many teenagers who are sexually active will not seek contraceptive services at all if they have to tell their parents first, either have no restriction on minors' access to contraception or have policies that define the conditions under which a minor can have access.

A majority of states require parental involvement—notification or consent—when a minor seeks abortion. The Supreme Court has ruled that parents may not have absolute veto power over a daughter's decision; still, many states require that one parent be involved. Some states allow a medical emergency exception and/or a judicial bypass, which allows a minor to obtain an abortion without parental involvement if a judge approves, or with the involvement of a parent-substitute, such as a grandparent.

How are children born to teenage mothers and to single mothers affected?

An important, ongoing longitudinal study, "The Fragile Families and Child Wellbeing Study," conducted jointly by research groups at Columbia and Princeton universities, shows that while half of unmarried parents are in "marriage-like" relationships and living with partners at the time of their child's birth, children born to unmarried parents are still more likely to grow up in poverty and not to fare as well as children born to married parents. For example, children living with unmarried mothers are likely to develop language skills more slowly and do less well on cognitive tests. Boys in these families are also likely to display more aggressive behavior than boys in families with married parents.[5]

Most studies do not explicitly compare the target population (children of unmarried parents) with children of divorced parents, for example, or with children of low-income married parents. But single mothers—including divorced, separated, or widowed mothers, as well as those never married—face the highest poverty rates (nearly 50 percent). It is difficult to distinguish whether this is because poor women have fewer opportunities to marry yet still want to become mothers, or whether the fact of having a child while unmarried causes poverty. We do know that poverty itself leads to problematic developmental outcomes for poor children and that being poor at birth is a strong predictor of future poverty status. Thirty-one percent of white children and 69 percent of black children who are poor at birth go on to spend at least half their childhoods living in poverty. In addition, children who are born into poverty and spend multiple years living in poor families have worse adult outcomes than their counterparts in higher-income families, such as more difficulty achieving employment and marital stability. Finally, the question remains, should low-income women refrain from having children or should social policies support a right of all women to reproduce, and assist those who for whatever reason need economic aid? These questions are particular important now as the child poverty rate in the United States has recently hit levels not seen since the 1960s.[6]

9

VALUES DEBATES AND REPRODUCTIVE POLITICS

What is "abstinence only" sex education?

In the 1980s, with high rates of abortion, pregnancy, and child-bearing outside of marriage, sexually transmitted diseases, and other evidence of teenagers engaging in sexual intercourse, many politicians and religious leaders became more vocal in promoting "abstinence only" education as a substitute for sex education in schools. Abstinence programs advocate no sex before marriage—and, on the whole, also omit any information about birth control, safe sex, and sexual orientation. During the administration of President George W. Bush, federal funding for "abstinence only" education grew rapidly.

Social scientists have tested the efficacy of "abstinence only" education, including a targeted evaluation sponsored by the US Department of Health and Human Services in 2007, and have found that such programs have actually not delayed sexual activity. The average age of "sexual debut" was the same for abstinence-until-marriage participants and control groups: fourteen years, nine months. Students who take "virginity pledges" while in the program end up much less likely to use contraception when they do become sexually active. Not surprisingly, then, as many educators and social scientists have pointed out, abstinence programs do not reduce rates of sexually transmitted diseases (STDs). In fact, education programs that withhold information about STDs, together with a medical care system that often does not test adolescents for these diseases, end up harming young people. (States with abstinence-only sex education policies have the highest rates of STDs among adolescents, and states with no mandates for abstinence had the lowest rates of infection among this group.) Forty percent of chlamydia cases (an STD that disproportionately affects women under twenty-five) result in pelvic inflammatory disease (PID) and one in five of the resultant cases of PID causes infertility, a condition that disproportionately affects poor and minority women.[1]

One recent study showed that inner-city middle school students in Philadelphia did delay their "sexual debuts" after having participated in an abstinence program, although the curriculum in this case did not focus on abstinence until marriage. Instead, it stressed comprehensive sex education and concepts like delaying sexual activity until maturity and promoted abstinence as a strategy for avoiding teen pregnancy and STDs rather than for moral or religious reasons. Similarly, in 2012, Mississippi decided to reassess its longtime commitment to "abstinence only" education when its teen pregnancy rate remained the highest in the nation.

The American Medical Association, American Public Health Association, the Society for Adolescent Medicine, and other major health organizations have all stated official support for comprehensive sex education designed to reduce sexually transmitted disease and out-of-wedlock or teenage pregnancies.

When did "life begins at conception" emerge as an important idea in reproductive politics?

Aristotle and St. Augustine both asserted that the human soul could not exist within an unformed body, a perspective that governed thinking about both the fetus and early abortion for centuries. In 1869, however, Pope Pius IX asserted the Catholic Church's censure of both early term and later abortions, and by the end of the nineteenth century, many American physicians engaged in the campaign to criminalize abortion argued that fetal life begins at fertilization. Nevertheless, for decades after that, US law associated "fetal personhood" with "viability," the point at which the fetus could live independently outside the woman's body.

In the mid-twentieth century, developments within the field of embryology clarified that fetal life predated fetal movement and that "viability" was merely one of a number of developmental stages. By 1960, in a significant legal turnaround, eighteen states had awarded damages in cases where a fetus had been harmed or killed, giving legal weight to the idea that fetal life was independent from the pregnant woman's life, even before viability. In the context of the Cold War and the ascendancy of Freudian-influenced cultural and psychological theories, a number of American writers associated the concept of the fetus as a person with key American values such as individualism and equality.[2] Also in this period, and particularly after *Roe v. Wade*, other religious groups in addition to Catholics, drawing on these medical, legal, and cultural developments, began to date "fetal personhood" at conception, not viability. When "fetal personhood" emerged as a concept, and technology provided fetal imagery, the anti-abortion platform increasingly denied a distinction between the "unborn" and the "born" and began to define abortion as murder.

What relationship does the anti-abortion movement claim with the nineteenth-century abolitionist movement?

Some proponents of the anti-abortion movement have claimed that their cause and the movement to end slavery are both freedom struggles. The fetal person, they argue, is a "slave in the womb," unfree due to unjust laws of a nation that denies the humanity of the fetus in the same way that laws justifying the slavery regime denied the full humanity of enslaved Africans. Some anti-abortion activists argue that both the beliefs and strategies of the nineteenth-century abolitionist movement are models for those working to end legal abortion, highlighting the religious and church-based aspects of both movements; the shared belief in the need to change a sinning culture through widespread conversion; and the use of strategic organizing around the country to achieve the movements' ends.

Additionally, the role of violence has been a point of debate within both movements. After the Fugitive Slave Law of 1850 was passed, many formerly pacifist abolitionists adopted the position that violence had a legitimate role in attacking the institution of slavery. When abolitionist John Brown, who advocated armed insurrection as a tactic for ending slavery, led the violent attack on the arsenal at Harpers Ferry in 1859, few abolitionists objected. Many accepted Brown's characterization of himself as an "avenging angel of the Lord." In the years after the legalization of abortion, over 1,800 anti-abortion activists committed violent attacks against abortion facilities and staff, claiming, like Brown, that violence was justified in the fight for a righteous cause, in the name of the country's salvation.

What is "Feminists for Life" (FFL)?

Feminists for Life, one of the first national anti-abortion organizations, was founded in 1972, soon after individual states began to overturn their anti-abortion statutes and the year before *Roe v. Wade.* FFL presents itself as pro-life and pro-women, and describes the group's mission as promoting progressive solutions for women and families and as standing for justice, nondiscrimination, and nonviolence. The core purpose of FFL is to oppose legal abortion and to eliminate social and economic conditions that press women to end their pregnancies. Every abortion, according to FFL, is a statement that American society has failed women, who, as a group, deserve better than to have to end a pregnancy.

Feminists for Life considers itself a nonpolitical organization. Though its anti-abortion position often puts it into alignment with conservative groups, its stance for enhanced public spending in the interests of mothers and children puts the organization at odds with those same groups. Abortion rights groups, while sometimes supporting public policies to enable poor women to reproduce if they choose to, question FFL's belief that a lack of adequate resources and support are the only grounds on which women decide to terminate a pregnancy and question whether it is possible to be a "feminist" with an agenda about what "all women" must do regarding any matter, including their fertility. Additionally, FFL places its anti-abortion position within the tradition of the sentiments of a great chain of early American feminists, such as Susan B. Anthony. Critics note, however, that Anthony and her contemporaries opposed abortion chiefly because they saw it as a practice undermining women's chastity, the preservation of which was one of women's few claims to moral authority—a distinctly nineteenth-century perspective.

How are attitudes and policies regarding gays and lesbians as parents evolving in the United States?

Americans' attitudes toward both homosexuality and families headed by same-sex or LGBTQI (lesbian, gay, bi-sexual, transgender, queer, intersex) persons have been trending positive for some years, especially among persons younger than thirty-five. Still, recent polls have shown that up to two-thirds of Americans do not consider a cohabiting same-sex couple raising children to constitute "a family," and at least half of Americans believe that states should not permit gays and lesbians to adopt (although Florida is the only state that bans adoption by same-sex couples). As of 2012, the District of Columbia and a growing group of states including Connecticut, New York, Iowa, Massachusetts, New Hampshire, Washington,

Maryland, Maine, and Vermont, allows same-sex marriage though in some of these states, the matter may not be settled.

Meanwhile, about one-quarter of same-sex couples are raising children. Some demographers suggest this involves as many as 9 million children in the United States. In recent years, courts have come to consider a parent's sexuality irrelevant in making a child-custody decision, and most recent academic studies have found no significant associations between sexual orientation and parenting skill or child adjustment.[3]

What is a "conscience clause"?

Almost all states allow individual health care providers and health care institutions the right to refuse to provide abortion services, although fifteen states allow private health care institutions alone this right. A small number of states including Arizona, Arkansas, Georgia, Idaho, Mississippi, and South Dakota allow pharmacists to refuse to provide services related to contraception; this provision often focuses on emergency contraception—that is, medication administered during a short period after unprotected sex. Almost one-third of the states allow health care providers to refuse to provide sterilization services. Many state legislatures continue to consider bills dealing with these matters, so laws governing provision of reproductive health services are continually shifting.

"Refusal" or "conscience" clauses allow providers to opt out of providing pharmaceuticals or services if doing so runs against their religious or moral beliefs. Laws permitting the opt-out are constitutionally valid because they are designed to accommodate the religious beliefs of providers, though the laws must include an exception if the woman's life or health is at risk. Most states (or boards that regulate pharmacists' professional conduct) require that if a pharmacist refuses to dispense contraceptives, he or she must refer the woman to another pharmacy. Conscience clauses can create a burden for women in rural areas with few reproductive health care providers and pharmacies, raising the possibility of an impermissible "undue burden." The courts have also dealt with questions about whether conscience clauses can constitute an undue hardship for a pharmacist's employer who might lose business because of the employee's refusal to dispense contraceptives. Opponents of conscience clauses also raise issues about whether, over time, providers of medical services might invoke such clauses to justify their refusal to provide care or medications in cases where they judge the illness—for example, a sexually transmitted infection—to have been contracted in the process of an activity they deem sinful.

10

CONTRACEPTION

What are the most commonly used forms of contraception in the United States?

Almost all heterosexual, sexually active women have used at least one form of contraception; nearly 90 percent of such women who do not want to get pregnant use contraception today. The pill (28 percent) and sterilization (27 percent) are the most commonly used methods of contraception in the United States. Women's decisions about which contraceptive method to use are associated in part with their race, class, marital status, and age. Women younger than thirty years of age and white women favor the pill; women older than thirty, women of color, and poor women are more likely to choose sterilization. Just under 10 percent of women have sex with men who have had vasectomies and just over 16 percent with men using condoms. About 5.5 percent of contraception-using women use an intrauterine device (IUD); 5.2 percent employ the withdrawal method; and 3.2 percent get injections every three months (Depo-Provera) to control fertility.[1]

Is "emergency contraception" the same thing as abortion?

The National Institutes of Health and the American College of Obstetricians and Gynecologists affirm that pregnancy occurs when a fertilized egg implants in the lining of a woman's uterus; implantation begins five to seven days after fertilization and takes several days. Emergency contraception, also called Plan B, will not work if the woman is already pregnant. Emergency contraception either delays or inhibits ovulation, interferes with fertilization by reducing the chance that the egg and sperm will meet, or prevents a fertilized egg from implanting in the uterine lining. All of these events antedate pregnancy. As of 2012, women at least seventeen years old can obtain emergency contraception without a prescription.

Why are long-acting contraceptives politically controversial?

Contraceptives such as Norplant (discontinued in 2002), an implant, and Depo-Provera, an injection, which provide protection against pregnancy and last three months or longer, became controversial in the 1990s soon after they were approved by the Federal Drug Administration (FDA). Controversy arose when some politicians, policy makers, and judges suggested or imposed the use of these drugs as a way of reducing welfare expenditures or required minority women appearing before the court to take a long-acting contraceptive in exchange for judicial leniency. At the same time, some clinics and schools in largely poor neighborhoods made these forms of birth control, and not others, available to young women for free. Opponents of long-acting methods charged that some women were pressed into using these contraceptives without a physician's opinion as to whether they were medically appropriate in any given case. Critics also charged that coercive uses of Depo-Provera and implantation methods revealed an official, late-twentieth-century bias that echoed earlier eugenic-based policies: targeting certain females for long-acting contraception supports the idea that motherhood in the United States is an economic status that should be reserved for financially secure, often white, women.

Why isn't there a male hormonal contraceptive?

Scientists began to conduct studies in this area in the 1950s, predicting success in the short term. It soon became clear, however, that men who used hormonal-based contraceptives would have to deal with unpleasant issues such as diminished sexual desire, the need to avoid alcohol, and potential health threats. In the 1960s and 1970s, in the context of feminist claims that men should share responsibility for contraception, widespread concern about "overpopulation," and the appearance of multiple problems associated with the female "pill," men increasingly used traditional methods such as condoms and vasectomies. Among men, enthusiasm for male contraceptives remained low as the new hormonal preparations proved problematic, variously causing testicles to shrink in size, diminished sex drive, impotence, and a male version of "hot flashes." Despite the feminist movement's emphasis on expansive concepts of gender roles and responsibilities, most men still seemed to believe that contraception was a women's job or duty. By the end of the twentieth century, a number of factors were responsible for delaying the development of the male hormonal contraceptive, including those based in male biology; the difficulty of raising money for research and attracting scientists and institutional support to this field; and problems with testing. Some experts have claimed that simple sexism has been a major factor in the delay, citing men's unwillingness to undergo the rigors and risks of using contraceptives that millions of women have built into their lives.

Is breast-feeding an effective contraceptive?

Medical experts say that breast-feeding is an effective method of contraception for the first six months after delivery because during continuous breast-feeding the woman's body produces a hormone that inhibits ovulation. This method of contraception is effective only if the baby is breast-fed every four hours during the day and every six hours at night, and if the baby takes no formula or other nourishment during these months.

Does the federal government pay for contraceptives and other reproduction-related services?

In 1970, Congress passed the Title X Family Planning program as part of the Public Health Service Act. Title X is the only federal grant program that provides comprehensive family planning and related health services, including access to contraceptive services, supplies, and information. The law indicates that priority is given to individuals with low incomes. By the end of the first decade in the twenty-first century, more than 5 million women and men were receiving services under Title X each year, including contraceptive services; patient education and counseling; breast and pelvic examinations; breast and cervical cancer screenings; STD and human immunovirus (HIV) education, testing, counseling, and referral; and pregnancy testing and counseling. No Title X funds are used for abortion services, nor may these funds be used in locations where abortion is provided.

Title X funds are disbursed to community-based clinics in a number of sites, from university health centers and tribal clinics, to faith-based organizations and other public and private nonprofit agencies. Politicians who do not support publicly funded reproductive health care have repeatedly targeted Title X, attempting to end all federal support for these sites and services.

In 1998, women's rights groups successfully championed legislation that guarantees all federal workers insurance coverage for contraceptive drugs and devices.[2]

What is the annual cost to US taxpayers of unintended pregnancies?

Almost half of all pregnancies in the United States each year are unintended. Recently, policy experts calculated the publicly financed costs associated with these pregnancies, including costs for abortion, fetal losses, births, and infant medical care. Overall, the study found that the total cost to US taxpayers was between $4.7 and $6.2 billion a year. The research analysts found that prevention of an unintended pregnancy would save the full cost of these services and prevention of a "mistimed" pregnancy (one that might occur later, under better circumstances for the pregnant woman and her partner) would save substantial, but less, taxpayer money.[3]

11

CONTEMPORARY ABORTION POLITICS I—OPINIONS AND SCIENCE

What are the most common objections to abortion today, and how have objections changed over time?

Objections to abortion have changed over time. In the nineteenth century, before antibiotics, many physicians favored outlawing abortion in order to protect pregnant women from infection and death. As we've seen, First Wave feminists spoke out against abortion as a threat to a woman's chastity and her moral authority, as well as to her husband's commitment to fidelity. In the mid-twentieth century, during trials of criminal abortion providers, the chief accusation against a woman who ended her pregnancy was that she failed to fulfill her destiny as a woman, that is, she murdered motherhood. In the illegal era (mid-nineteenth century until 1973), anti-abortion arguments focused much more directly on the pregnant woman than they do today, when the most common objection to abortion is based on the claim that life begins at conception, so abortion is murder. Opposition to abortion today generally focuses directly on the life of the "unborn child," giving its interests and potentialities greater weight than the circumstances, the decisions, and sometimes even the life of the pregnant woman. The requirement of a civilized society to prevent murder trumps all other considerations, according to this view.

People who believe that abortion constitutes murder often suggest that adoption is a reasonable and fruitful alternative to abortion, as adoption allows the child to live and also provides a baby for others who may not be able, themselves, to reproduce.

The anti-abortion view also warns that abortion is dangerous to a woman's health, claiming that women who have abortions are more likely to have medical complications and encounter psychological problems later in life, although medical research has not been able to validate these claims.

How do advocates of abortion rights make their case?

Abortion rights advocates argue that the fertilized egg and its subsequent forms during the early stages of pregnancy (weeks 1–12, the period when approximately 90 percent of abortions in the United States are performed)[1] represent potential life, but not a person or a separate entity capable of living independently of the woman. Therefore, they argue, abortion does not constitute the murder of a person any more than discarding an unimplanted fertilized egg after an in vitro procedure does.

Abortion rights arguments also stress that a woman's right to manage her own body, including her fertility, is crucial to her status as a full citizen. Historically, they argue, when the government has taken the right to force women to stay pregnant, it has also taken the right to deny women contraception, to force some women to get sterilized, and to support treating the reproductive capacity of different groups of women differently, depending on their race and class. All of these practices have degraded women in the past, compromising their ability to live dignified and autonomous lives.

Rights advocates argue that *Roe v. Wade* legalized abortion, so abortion is a woman's right, and that women are capable of making their own decisions about exercising their rights without state-mandated education requirements or other constraints designed to discourage abortion. While *Roe v. Wade* does not address sex equality, a number of feminist scholars and others have argued that the abortion right is best conceptualized in a sex equality framework.

What do public opinion polls show about American attitudes toward abortion today?

Opinion polls in the last decade show substantial swings in levels of support and opposition for abortion. Recent polls have shown that 54 percent of Americans believe that abortion should be legal in all or most cases; 39 percent oppose abortion in all or most cases.[2] As in earlier periods, most people who regularly attend religious services are anti-abortion, and the majority of those who rarely or never attend services support abortion rights. Polls have found that fewer Americans believed that abortion is a "critical issue" in 2010 than in 2006, but with a pro-choice president elected in 2008 and many state legislatures in the control of Republicans after the 2010 elections, the push for anti-abortion legislation at the state level has been vigorous.

Is there evidence that abortion causes psychological and physical illness, and deleteriously affects subsequent pregnancies?

Johns Hopkins University researchers recently conducted a comprehensive review of the scientific literature concerning the impact of abortion on a woman's mental health. The review found that "the highest-quality research available does not support the hypothesis that abortion leads to long-term mental health problems."[3] Likewise, a recent report by the American Psychological Association's (APA) Task Force on Mental Health and Abortion concluded that among women with unplanned pregnancies, the risk of mental health problems is no greater for those who obtain a first trimester abortion than among those who carry the pregnancy to term. In general, studies have found that those who have had an abortion report a broad range of emotions. Relief is the most commonly reported emotion, although some women also report sadness or guilt. Evidence indicates that some women suffer because of the stigma associated with abortion rather than from the abortion itself.[4]

Neither the APA nor the American Psychiatric Association recognizes the "post-abortion traumatic stress syndrome," or "post-abortion trauma," first defined in 1981 by psychotherapist Vincent Rue as a mental health consequence for women who obtain abortions. Despite the scientific evidence, many opponents of abortion continue to claim that "post-abortion trauma" is an inevitable consequence for most women and use this claim to try to convince women that abortion will harm them.

One serious problem in this domain is that most people are not trained to distinguish between the findings of studies that are rigorous methodologically and those that are not. The most scientifically reliable work, from which legitimate conclusions can be drawn, such as the Johns Hopkins study, isolates the *effects* of abortion. Less reliable studies may show only *associations* between abortion and mental health outcomes. The APA has found that the majority of studies of the psychological impacts of abortion suffer from methodological flaws including the lack of a comparison group and sample sizes that are too small to allow generalization to the population at large; failure to control for preexisting conditions that might account for later mental health problems and failure to account for the fact that many women do not admit to having had one or more abortions; and the use of imprecise or insufficient methods to assess mental health outcomes.

In the 1990s, some anti-abortion proponents claimed an association between abortion and breast cancer. In 2003 the National Cancer Institute (NCI) convened a group of 100 of the world's leading experts on the subject who concluded that having an abortion or miscarriage does not increase a woman's chances of contracting breast cancer.

NCI has explained that studies in the past, both those that suggested some link or no link between abortion and breast cancer, were flawed in various ways and are therefore unreliable. Today, better-designed studies, using an adequate number of women reporting on their pregnancy histories before they were diagnosed with breast cancer, as well as other high-quality methodological features, yield reliable findings. NCI reports that "the newer studies consistently showed no association between induced and spontaneous abortion and breast cancer risk."[5]

Similarly, contemporary studies have found that abortions performed in the first trimester pose virtually no long-term risk of infertility, ectopic pregnancy, congenital malformation, miscarriage, or preterm or low-weight delivery.

12

CONTEMPORARY ABORTION POLITICS II—EXPERIENCE AND PRACTICE

What is the abortion rate in the United States and how has it changed in recent years?

After 1990, the number and rate of abortions declined every year for about a decade and a half, but recently, the number of abortions nationally has held steady, at around 1.2 million a year. The rate is highest in the Northeast (27 abortions per 1,000 women) and lowest in the Midwest (14 per 1,000). About 22 percent of all pregnancies end in abortion.[1]

At how many weeks of pregnancy is the typical abortion performed?

Almost 90 percent of abortions are performed within the first trimester of pregnancy—the first twelve weeks. About 1.5 percent are performed at twenty-one weeks of pregnancy or beyond. Anti-abortion advocates have claimed that women who get later abortions are simply behaving capriciously, but women may seek later abortions for a number of reasons. Tests results for genetic and health anomalies may not be available until after the first trimester. Also, some women who do not want to be pregnant discover late that they are and have trouble locating and accessing abortion services. Nearly 60 percent of those who delayed obtaining an abortion experienced difficulty raising the money to pay for the service and to make arrangements and pay for travel to practitioners at a distance from their home The majority of abortion patients today are low-income women for whom it can take a considerable period to raise the money for the procedure. Many low-income women do not have health insurance, live in one of the thirty-three states that do not help poor women pay for abortions, or live in states that otherwise severely restrict abortion coverage for public employees or via rules governing private insurance plans. Recent studies have affirmed that women face these and other challenges, including uncertainty about the date of the last menstrual period—a common problem for teenagers, who are more likely than older women to delay abortion until after 15 weeks.

What is the difference between a medical and a surgical abortion?

A medical abortion is performed only in the first trimester of pregnancy. The woman takes a medication—Mifepristone, orally, or Methotrexate, usually injected. Both drugs interrupt the process of implantation of the zygote in the uterine wall. Before implantation the woman's body does not receive the hormonal messages that trigger pregnancy. Another drug, Misoprostol, is taken orally or inserted vaginally within a few days after administration of the Mifepristone or Methotrexate, causing uterine contractions and increasing the effectiveness of the procedure. A medical abortion, which can be done at home in private, very early in pregnancy, resembles a "natural" or "spontaneous" miscarriage. A medical abortion is completed without the use of any surgical instruments, so the woman does not incur surgical risk of injury to the cervix or uterus or risks associated with anesthesia. On the other hand, a medical abortion requires at least two visits to the abortion practitioner; the procedure lasts for several days or more, and can, like some miscarriages, be very painful. Bleeding after the procedure may last longer than with a surgical abortion. As legislatures pile restrictions on a woman's access to surgical abortion, such as pre-abortion "education" sessions and waiting periods, the number of medical abortions has grown. In 2005, 161,000 women obtained medical abortions; in 2008, the number was 199,000. State legislatures have begun to develop strategies for limiting medical abortions.

A surgical abortion, usually preformed in the first trimester, is typically performed using a method called "vacuum aspiration": the cervix is gradually opened and a suction apparatus is inserted through the cervix into the uterus. The contents of the uterus are emptied by suction. This procedure requires one visit to the provider and takes only few minutes but still carries the risks of surgery and does not allow the kind of privacy that a medical abortion does.

What is the difference between a D&X procedure, a "partial birth" abortion, a "late-term" abortion, and a "later" abortion?

A "D&X procedure" (standing for "dilate and extract"), also known as an "intact D&E" or "intrauterine cranial decompression" procedure, is a rare and more invasive type of abortion, usually performed in the fifth month of gestation or later. In this kind of abortion, the fetus's head is compressed before its body is removed from the womb, to minimize the damage to the woman. Contrary to opponents' claims, the D&X procedure is performed very rarely and almost exclusively in cases where the physician, facing a severe medical emergency, determines that this procedure presents the least harm to the woman and does not end her capacity to bear children. These circumstances include cases in which genetic tests, the results of which become available late in the second trimester, show serious problems; when the fetus is dead; when the fetus is alive but the pregnancy threatens the woman's life; or when the fetus is so damaged that it will not live after birth.

D&X procedures are sometimes called "partial birth abortions," but this is not a medical term. Rather, it is a term created by anti-abortion groups as a tactic for capturing the horror of a rare abortion procedure which, using variously restrictive language and laws, has been banned in over thirty states. All states have enacted some kind of exception to the ban in situations where a woman's life or health is at stake, although not all the exceptions are in effect.

Many physicians approve of and use the term "later abortion" to identify any pregnancy termination after seventeen weeks of gestational age. The mainstream media and lay people use a variety of terms, including "late-term abortion," and those in the field may employ the terms "second-trimester abortion" and "mid-trimester abortion." Generally states cannot ban abortion even after fetal viability if the procedure is necessary to preserve the life or the physical or mental health of the woman, as determined by the woman's physician, who also has the latitude to determine the viability of the fetus. In 2007, however, the Supreme Court upheld the federal Partial-Birth Abortion Ban Act of 2003, which imposes fines or imprisonment or both on a physician who performs a "partial birth abortion;" the act includes no health exception.

How safe is abortion, generally?

Abortion complications are rare; public health data show that fewer than 0.3 percent of abortion patients experience a complication that requires hospitalization. Death from abortion is also rare, although abortion becomes increasingly dangerous as the pregnancy progresses. Before eight weeks' gestation, the risk of death is one in a million abortions. Between sixteen and twenty weeks, the death rate is one in 29,000, and after twenty-one weeks, when, by far the fewest abortions take place, the rate is one per 11,000 abortions.[2]

Who obtains abortions in the United States today?

In the United States, as stated earlier, almost half of all pregnancies are unintended and about 40 percent of these unintended pregnancies are ended by abortion. Every year, among women from fifteen to forty-four years of age in the United States, about 2 percent have an abortion, and about half of these women have had an earlier abortion. According to the Guttmacher Institute, at least half of American women will have an untended pregnancy before menopause, and about one-third will have had an abortion by age forty-five.[3]

The following characteristics describe women who obtain abortions today:

Teenagers	18 percent of all abortions
Ages 21–29	58 percent
Identify as Protestant	37 percent
Identify as Catholic	28 percent
Religiously affiliated	73 percent
Non-Hispanic Black	30 percent
Non-Hispanic White	36 percent
Never married, not cohabiting	45 percent
Mothers of one or more children	61 percent
Very low income (Incomes between 100% and 199% of poverty level)	69 percent

What are some reasons women give for having abortions?

Too many existing responsibilities	75 percent
Cannot afford a child	75 percent
Must work, go to school, care for dependents	75 percent
Doesn't want to be a single parent	50 percent
Not in stable relationship	50 percent

Why is the abortion rate so high for poor women?

Even though black and white women report wanting the same number of children, black women are three times as likely as white women to have an unintended pregnancy. Hispanic women are about twice as likely as white women to become accidentally pregnant. Still, abortion rates have been falling for African Americans since 2000, declining 18 percent over that period. The startling demographic fact is that women with incomes less than 100 percent of the federal poverty level get about 40 percent of all abortions in the United States.

Public health research finds that poor women, especially poor women of color, have more trouble than other women accessing high-quality reproductive health care, particularly contraceptive services. Anti-abortion restrictions and cuts to publicly funded family-planning services have particularly harsh impacts on these women. Many poor women live in areas characterized by inadequate reproductive health services and few transportation options. Also, when poor women do access contraceptive services, they are often unable to afford the most effective methods of birth control and end up relying on condoms and other less reliable methods. This leads to high rates of unintended pregnancies, which are closely associated with high rates of abortion. Studies also find that the association of abortion and poverty is built upon additional factors such as the ways that poverty contributes to limited access to information; to unstable life situations; to pervasive mistrust of the health care system generally, including reproductive health care providers. Other barriers to sensitive and responsive health care delivery are cultural and linguistic.[4]

How many abortion practitioners provide services in the United States today, and how are their services distributed geographically?

At the end of the first decade of the twenty-first century, there were just under 1,800 abortion practitioners in the United States, a number that has been declining for the past three decades although it is currently holding steady. Analysts have estimated that the number of abortion providers declined 25 percent between 1992 and 2008. Also, physicians who perform abortions are an aging group; about 63 percent are fifty years old or older.

Eighty-seven percent of all US counties do not have an abortion provider; 35 percent of all women of childbearing age live in these counties. The percentage of counties without practitioners varies according to the region of the country. For example, in the Northeast, 53 percent of the counties lack an abortion provider; 18 percent of women of childbearing age in the Northeast live in those counties. Abortion providers are concentrated in cities, but 69 percent of counties in metropolitan areas do not have abortion providers. Women who live in rural areas are the most isolated from abortion service: 97 percent of non-metropolitan counties lack providers. In South Dakota, for example, no resident physician performs abortions; instead, physicians from Minnesota fly to the state weekly to perform the procedure.

A 2010 study showed that many physicians who plan to provide abortion services and receive training for this specialty in residency programs ultimately cannot realize their plans because of formal and informal policies restricting abortion provision by their private group practices, employers, and hospitals.[5]

In what settings are abortions typically performed?

Freestanding abortion clinics and other clinics provide the vast majority of all abortions, roughly 94 percent. Only about 4 percent of abortions are performed in hospitals and 1 percent in physicians' offices.[6]

After *Roe v. Wade*, many hospitals indicated their determination not to provide abortions. One year after *Roe*, no Catholic hospitals provided abortions; 30 percent of other non-voluntary hospitals (private, for-profit hospitals that do not provide free care to the poor) and 15 percent of municipal hospitals provided the service. Consequently, physicians opened freestanding abortion clinics in cities and towns around the country, a development that underwrote the emergence of women-centered practices but also facilitated precisely targeted anti-abortion activities.

Are abortion practitioners in danger today?

Between 1977 and 2009, the National Abortion Federation, using statistics compiled and classified by law enforcement agencies, recorded 6,263 incidents against abortion providers categorized as "violence," 163,744 acts of "disruption," and 763 "clinic blockades." Acts of violence include murder (8), bombings (41), arson (175), anthrax threats (661), death threats (416), vandalism (1,429), and stalking (526).

In 2009, Scott Roeder, an anti-abortion activist, murdered Dr. George Tiller, an abortion practitioner in Wichita, Kansas, who had been stalked, threatened, and otherwise harassed for many years. Sixteen years earlier, Dr. Tiller had been shot in both arms outside of his clinic. Dr. Tiller was the fourth doctor killed by anti-abortion extremists; the others murdered included clinic employees, a security guard, and a volunteer clinic escort.

Many people who oppose legal abortion also profoundly oppose violence against abortion doctors and their staffs and facilities. Still, the constant, public characterization of abortion as murder and abortion practitioners as murderers has, for some extremists, justified killing staff at abortion clinics. In this context, anti-abortion extremists continue to deliver death threats to physicians and commit acts of vandalism at abortion clinics. In recent years, 88 percent of abortion clinics experienced at least one of six forms of harassment; 87 percent were picketed. Providers in the South and Midwest were the most likely to experience harassment (75 percent and 85 percent, respectively).[7] Between January and May 2012, abortion facilities in and around Atlanta, Georgia, were targeted, with at least five incidents of building fires and burglaries.

Unsurprisingly, violence and disruption targeting abortion providers has caused some practitioners to leave the field, especially in the South and the Midwest. Recent research, however, challenges the idea that violence and threats of violence are the chief force driving some physicians and staff from the field, suggesting instead that hospital and group practice policies make abortion practice impossible for some physicians who want to provide abortions.

Do medical schools teach abortion practice?

Ninety seven percent of family practice residents and 36 percent of obstetrics and gynecology (Ob/Gyn) residents have no experience in first-trimester abortion procedures. Indeed, a recent study found that abortion education is limited in medical schools in the United States. The authors of the study sent a questionnaire to the relevant program directors at the 126 accredited medical schools in the the country; 62 percent of the questionnaires (from 78 medical schools) were completed and returned. Based on the data available, the authors found that a minority of medical education programs offered abortion education at any level of medical training. Even when clinical experience was offered as part of third-year rotations (45 percent reported the availability of this experience), participation was low, suggesting to the authors that medical faculty did not encourage student proficiency in this area, and possibly suggesting that students avoided abortion training as a stigmatized, dangerous, or impossibly constrained field.[8]

Indicating the breadth of intentions of anti-abortion legislators, in 2011 the US Congress passed a bill forbidding federal funds from being used to teach medical students how to perform abortions, a proposal that, if it ever became law, would leave physicians without training that they might certainly need in an emergency, even if abortion were criminalized.

13

CONTEMPORARY ABORTION III—ACTIVISM, LAW, AND POLICY

*How are state legislatures responding to abortion
and satellite issues?*

In recent years many state legislatures have defined abortion and efforts to limit the procedure as their number one social issue. In fact, the state legislature, rather than Congress or the courts, has become the chief venue for pro-life activism and action in the United States. Hundreds of abortion-limitation bills have been introduced in legislatures around the country, and a number have become law. Legislation has focused on eliminating all state funding for abortions or clinics that provide abortion counseling and services; limiting abortion coverage by private insurers; enforcing special qualifications for performing abortions and onerous and irrelevant requirements regarding sites where the procedure may be performed. Many state legislatures have created more expansive rules governing the right to refuse to perform and participate in abortions. New laws mandate special pre-abortion counseling, including counseling by nonmedical personnel, ultrasound imaging, waiting periods, and parental involvement in the case of minors seeking abortion. Other laws forbid telemedicine abortions, which allow a physician from a "remote" location to guide a women through a nonsurgical and medical (taking an oral prescription drug) abortion.[1]

What is pre-abortion counseling?

This term refers to a state requirement that clinic staff, including medical staff, provide an abortion-seeking woman with literature or other materials that state legislators have decided she must have. Generally, state-mandated "pre-abortion counseling" does not meet traditional definitions of counseling in which a credentialed counselor takes part in a therapeutic give-and-take with a person seeking assistance. Under this law, the woman must receive such counseling whether she wants exposure to this material or not, in order to decide whether to go forward with the procedure.

As I pointed out earlier, more than thirty states require that women receive counseling before undergoing an abortion procedure, and more than twenty prescribe the kind of information that the client must receive, including material about fetal development, adoption alternatives, and state laws that require fathers to contribute to child support. Some states allow the curriculum to include a presentation about the possible relationship between abortion and breast cancer, for which scientific proof does not exist. Some states use the pre-abortion counseling experience as an opportunity to dissuade women from going ahead with the abortion, focusing only on negative psychological outcomes.

Critics of pre-abortion counseling curricula raise questions about whether states have the right to interrupt the privileged relationship between the patient and the doctor. Critics are concerned about the ways that the curricula compromise a woman's right to make a decision on her own; about how the curricula interfere with the doctor's right to manage his medical practice; and about how the curricula distort the "informed consent" process.

Abortion-rights advocates have argued in court that most pre-abortion counseling curricula constitute an "undue burden" on a woman seeking an abortion, but courts have not agreed, ruling against constitutional challenges and allowing the counseling to continue. By 2006, anti-abortion counseling centers had more than $60 million in federal funds, and twenty states had designated funding for such centers, a dozen states raising funds with "Choose Life" license plates.

What are "waiting periods"?

Mandatory delay laws or "waiting periods" require women to wait for a prescribed period of time (usually twenty-four hours, but at least one state, Utah, has passed a law requiring a seventy-two-hour period) between receiving state-mandated information about the procedure at an abortion clinic and having the abortion. State legislation mandates these waiting periods under the theory that a woman who spends the interval thinking about what she has learned during pre-abortion counseling sessions will be less likely to go ahead with the procedure. Critics of waiting periods note that such delays often mean that women must make two trips from home to the clinic. The extra trip, particularly in parts of the country where women may have to travel significant distances from home to clinic, can require women to lose work time twice and to incur twice the travel and child-care expenses, or require funds to stay at a hotel near the clinic. Policies that require two trips thus significantly raise the cost of obtaining an abortion and may cause some women to delay the procedure and encounter the elevated risks that accompany later abortion.

What are TRAP laws?

Some states have passed laws mandating that medical practices of physicians who perform abortions must meet standards that are much stricter than those applied to other medical practices. These laws are called Targeted Regulation of Abortion Providers, or TRAP laws; this term is typically used within the reproductive rights movement. The laws often require that facilities undergo expensive renovations or incorporate architectural changes that are impossible or unnecessary. They may also include standards for staffing and procedures that are not applied to any other kind of practice. An abortion provider may be required to become licensed as an "ambulatory surgical center (ASC)," that is, a facility that provides many kinds of out-patient surgeries, even though only first-trimester abortions are performed in the setting. This is, again, an expensive proposition and one not recommended by standard-setting national health organizations.

These and other state mandates included in TRAP laws can make performing abortions too expensive and burdensome for physicians, causing some to close their practices. The Center for Reproductive Rights has found TRAP laws very difficult to oppose in court, although recently attorneys associated with the Center reached an agreement with the state of Missouri exempting a physician who had been providing abortions for thirty years from meeting new ASC regulations.

What is the Freedom of Access to Clinic Entrances (FACE) Act?

In the sixteen years between 1977 and 1993, anti-abortion protesters conducted 609 blockades around the country, preventing women from gaining access to abortion clinics. At the end of this period, Dr. David Gunn of Florida became the first provider to be shot and killed; a number of arson attacks were also carried out against clinics that year. In response, with solid bi-partisan support, Congress passed the FACE Act which was signed into law by President Clinton in 1994.

The act forbids assaults on an abortion-providing facility, its clients, or personnel, including by the use of "force, threat of force or physical obstruction to intentionally injure, intimidate, interfere with" anyone who is performing or obtaining reproductive health services. Anyone who violates the Freedom of Access to Clinic Entrances Act faces both civil and criminal penalties. For the sixteen years following enactment of the federal FACE Act, the total number of blockades fell by about 75 percent, compared to the earlier period.

What is a Crisis Pregnancy Center?

Approximately 4,000 sites in the United States, known as crisis pregnancy centers (CPCs), reach out to women who are accidentally pregnant, pregnant without resources, or fear that they are pregnant. Center staff generally offer counseling about the importance of keeping the pregnancy and talk to clients about alternatives to both abortion and motherhood and related subjects. Generally, crisis pregnancy centers have a religiously imbued, anti-abortion mission. Some centers employ part-time medical staff and offer ultrasound imaging.

Critics charge that CPCs—many of which receive state and federal support—advertise their services, locate and outfit their offices, and target unsuspecting clients in ways that suggest the facilities offer comprehensive services of all kinds, including contraceptive services and abortion, while obfuscating or misrepresenting their core purpose: to discourage abortion. Austin, Texas; Baltimore, Maryland; and New York City have each enacted legislation that requires crisis pregnancy centers to post notices informing prospective clients whether they have medical personnel on staff and that the center does not provide abortion services or referrals to clinics that provide these services.

Can women use health insurance plans to cover abortion?

Although complete information is difficult to obtain, the best information available—from Guttmacher Institute and Kaiser Family Foundations studies—suggests that most Americans who have employer-based health insurance have coverage of abortion.

A recent Guttmacher Institute study found that only about 30 percent of abortion patients had private insurance, one of a number of indications that a disproportionately high percentage of women seeking abortion today are low income. About one-third of the women who had private coverage used their insurance to pay for the abortion and just under two-thirds paid out of pocket. Private insurance paid for only about 12 percent of abortions, perhaps because many women did not know that their insurance plans covered abortion, or because a number of the women were covered by plans that excluded abortion. Possibly a number of the women in the study paid directly for the abortion because they had not yet met their plans' annual deductible amount. Some women, feeling stigmatized by their decision, may have paid out of pocket to avoid reporting their abortion to anyone, including the insurance company.

The future of insurance coverage for abortion is unclear due to the determination of anti-abortion activists to achieve Henry Hyde's goal of excluding coverage for women of all income levels. Congress and state legislatures have focused on creating restrictions that would affect millions of women who purchase insurance on state insurance exchanges, thereby making access to both private and public abortion insurance difficult or impossible to obtain.

What is the future of legal abortion?

With *Roe v. Wade*, state anti-abortion statutes were nullified and abortion became legal nationally. For abortion to be recriminalized in the twenty-first century, the United States Supreme Court would have to overturn *Roe v. Wade*. Under the legal principle stare decisis (a Latin term meaning, "to stand by that which is decided"), the legal status of abortion has been settled by *Roe v. Wade*, establishing a precedent that has force and duration—of forty years. Yet precedent does not always prevail. Courts may overturn long-standing laws, as social, political, cultural, and legal attitudes change over time.

For many years, the Supreme Court justices' attitudes toward abortion have been watched closely. It would take five justices to overturn *Roe v. Wade*. If this were to happen, the legal status of abortion would be defined by each of the fifty state legislatures, many of which have long been involved in crafting legislation to restrict abortion access. Also, some states, such as Rhode Island and Alabama, have never expunged from their books nineteenth-century laws criminalizing abortion. In states where courts have enjoined these laws, government lawyers could simply move to lift the bans on them, and the old laws would go back into effect. Experts have predicted that if *Roe v. Wade* is overturned, approximately thirty states, where about 50 percent of women in America live, would recriminalize abortion within a year. In the meantime, state legislatures are enacting a variety of laws that aim to sharply curtail access to abortion and constrain the ability of doctors to perform the procedure.

What does the abortion rights movement look like today?

As mentioned, recent polls show that more Americans believe that abortion should be legal in most or all cases than those who believe that abortion should be illegal in most or all cases. Nevertheless, after the 2010 elections, when Republicans took or maintained control of twenty-six state legislatures, states focused unprecedented attention on passing legislation concerning reproductive issues. The majority of these laws aim to restrict women's access to abortion, requiring extensive pre-abortion waiting periods, education, and imaging; regulating clinics as if they were hospitals; and forbidding private health insurance companies from covering abortion in almost all cases. Other laws deal with infant abandonment, still-birth certificates, sex education, and other issues; few have dealt with expanding women's access to reproductive health services.

The legal arm of the reproductive rights movement has focused on bringing suits challenging many of these laws. In particular, they have fought against laws that reduce women's overall access to reproductive health care; laws requiring women to receive pre-abortion counseling that may promote unsubstantiated connections between abortion and various subsequent diseases; and laws that make the most common type of abortion—first trimester procedures—harder to obtain because of very long waiting periods and insurance restrictions, among other new obstacles.

In addition to opposing anti-abortion legislation, mainstream reproductive rights organizations have focused in recent years on developing robust campus-based activist groups. Women-of-color organizations are leading educational efforts to expand the reproductive rights agenda beyond the abortion issue and to define reproductive rights as a human right, encompassing both the right of all women to be mothers if they so choose, and the right of women to manage their fertility. These groups, calling for "reproductive justice," focus on issues of reproductive health; comprehensive sex education; access to living wage jobs, decent housing, and affordable, high-quality day care; and other resources necessary for safe and dignified childbearing. Some groups in the contemporary reproductive health, rights, and justice movements are focusing on building coalitions with other rights-and-justice oriented organizations, such as civil, environmental, health care, and disability rights groups.

14

FETUSES

Has the fetus always been the focus of anti-abortion concerns?

Anti-abortion campaigns in the illegal era focused on a number of issues, from protecting women against life-endangering abortifacients and procedures; to the threatening association of abortion, illicit sexuality, and degraded chastity; to errant husbands, enabled by abortion to have sex outside of marriage without consequences. Physicians often focused their support of anti-abortion laws on the maligned figure of the unprofessional, mercenary abortion-performing midwife, determined to strip them of medical legitimacy and any right to minister to pregnant women. Others stressed how abortion contributed alarmingly to the falling birthrate among white, Protestant women. Increasingly in the pre-*Roe* period, champions of criminal abortion laws focused on how abortion "murdered motherhood," that is, alienated women from their true calling. When abortion practitioners were put on trial during the criminal era, whatever the state law said about causing the death of a "quickened" or "unquickened" fetus, quite often other issues apart from the potential child represented the chief concerns and subjects of interrogation in the courtroom.

While state legislatures in the nineteenth century were enacting anti-abortion statutes, attitudes about the nature of the fetus varied across professions. In scientific laboratories, for example, embryologists were constructing the embryo as a discrete specimen to be studied. In the courtroom, several important cases, including one (*Dietrich v. Northampton*, 1884) that came before Oliver Wendell Holmes, then chief justice of the Massachusetts State Supreme Court, found that the fetus was *not* a discrete individual because it was not indivisible from the mother.

Beginning in the 1920s, American law and culture began to disregard Holmes's dicta, finding that the fetus was, indeed, an independent being for which the pregnant woman simply provided food and shelter. Regarding the fetus as an "individual," many Americans began to picture the fetus as an expressive, didactic symbol imbued with a complex range of twentieth-century American values, concerns, and ideals.

Reinforcing this idea of the fetus as an independent, value-laden entity was the emergence of medical fetal imaging, as well as the publication of Lennart Nilsson's fetal photographs in LIFE magazine in 1965. Nilsson used a scanning electron microscope and other new photographic technologies to make images of hugely magnified, free-floating fetuses. (Neither the woman carrying the fetus nor any of her body parts were visible as such in the photographs.) Many viewers looked at these new kinds of images and perceived the fetus as a fully autonomous entity. At the same time as the fetus began to appear in this way, women's rights advocates, proponents of population control, physicians, and others began to support the right to abortion. The resulting collision between the champions of the fetus and the champions of women's rights led, through *Roe v. Wade*, to modern abortion politics, with its theological, biological, and rights content, all contributing in various ways to debates about the significance of fetal life.

What is "fetal personhood"?

The *Roe v. Wade* decision found that the fetus is not a legal "person" for the purposes of constitutional protection. In this, *Roe v. Wade* was consistent historically with both English common law and US law, which had always centered legal rights on the pregnant woman and did not construct the fetus as a person with full rights. In the wake of *Roe v. Wade*, anti-abortion activists drew attention to the vulnerable fetus, which required protection from harm or death, and began the process of blurring all distinctions between the fetus and the baby after birth. A significant aspect of anti-abortion activism has been to promote regulations and laws that define the responsibilities of pregnant women for their fetuses, ensuring that they are similar to a mother's responsibilities for her child. Today, an increasing number of state rules and laws defining and governing a pregnant woman's behaviors and duties construct the fetus as a person, due the kinds of statutory protections accorded a child.

What does "fetal rights" mean?

As anti-abortion advocates constructed the fetus as a "person," the same as a child, and defined the interests of the fetus as distinct from and perhaps in conflict with the interests of the pregnant woman, the fetus began to accrue the rights of an individual in society. Experts have identified three major areas in which "fetal rights" can be asserted and can prevail in court in ways that may eclipse the pregnant woman's needs, desires, rights, or even her life.

The first area emerged in part as a result of the developing practice of fetal medicine. Here, typically, a hospital obtains a court order that *requires* medical intervention in the interests of the well-being, perhaps even the survival, of the fetus, even though such an intervention might compromise the pregnant woman's desires, needs, rights, or well-being. For example, an obstetrician might tell a woman in labor that she requires a cesarean delivery or a transfusion, which for religious or other reasons, the woman rejects. The physician may decide that the pregnant woman is inappropriately or illegally putting her own needs or desires before the fetus's and obtain a court order to force the woman to go forward with the medical procedure that the physician recommends. When women have brought suit against authorities who forced them to have cesarean deliveries or transfusions, some courts have settled cases in favor of the fetus's right to be born in a healthy state, while others have upheld pregnant women's rights to refuse medical treatment.

Fetal rights have also been invoked in the workplace. For example, pregnant or fertile women have been excluded from jobs that involve contact with substances present in the worksite that might injure a fetus. In these cases, largely fought between the 1970s and the 1990s, businesses have claimed that fetuses must be protected from toxic materials. Because any premenopausal or unsterilized woman could theoretically be pregnant, company policy dictated that all fertile women must be ineligible for the sometimes higher-paying jobs that could potentially endanger the fetus, regardless of whether any given woman chose to work under those conditions. Some female employees argued that workplace policies concerned with the right of the fetus to be protected from toxic substances inappropriately treated all women as potentially pregnant and second-guessed the judgments of female employees, while ignoring the business's responsibility to provide a healthy work environment for all employees, male and female, pregnant and not.

Finally, the law has recognized fetal rights in cases involving the use of controlled substances by pregnant women. Such behavior is often called "fetal abuse," a term that links the charge to the well-recognized arena of child abuse and blurs distinction between the fetus and the child. Most pregnant women charged with fetal abuse are poor women of color and most prosecutions have involved cocaine, although medical research shows that alcohol and cigarette use in pregnancy are far more prevalent and cause much more severe harm to fetuses. Because most detoxification programs in the United States do not accept pregnant women, poor women in particular have very limited access to treatment for addiction while they are far more vulnerable to charges of violating a fetus's right to safety. Low-income women are especially vulnerable to targeting by medical facilities that have involuntary testing policies or by law enforcement agencies that arrest drug-using pregnant women on charges of fetal abuse. Also, most poor women do not have access to the resources required to obtain legal advice or representation when they are charged with fetal abuse, making this group simultaneously the most likely to be prosecuted and the least able to defend themselves.

Generally, critiques of "fetal rights" have focused on two related areas. First, critics have claimed that this concept has been used against pregnant women in ways that violate constitutional protections. They explain that surely, under some circumstance, it may be appropriate to advise a pregnant woman to change her behavior in the interests of fetal well-being. Nevertheless, when a pregnant woman is charged with violating fetal rights, typically her own access to equal treatment under the law is violated. This is because in such a case, the pregnant woman is assumed to have an obligation based on the rights of the fetus to submit to medical treatment, such as surgery or a blood transfusion, which is not imposed on others who are not pregnant and who are free to reject treatment. Proponents of the rights of pregnant women point out that society doesn't require a mother to donate one of her organs to her ill or dying child, another indication that the law treats pregnant women differently from other persons, violating this group's access to equal treatment under the law. Additionally, though prosecutors in such cases claim that the fetus and the child are indistinguishable regarding basic rights, the fetus (sometimes referred to as "the unborn child" or "the pre-born child") is actually accorded more rights than a child after he or she is born.

The second critique of fetal rights is that this issue has focused attention too narrowly on the alleged conflict between the rights and interests of the pregnant woman and the fetus, eclipsing the larger, structural causes of problematic behaviors and outcomes associated with pregnancy and childbearing in the United States. Some legal experts and advocates for the rights of pregnant women have pointed out that focusing on the alleged conflict between the rights of pregnant women and fetuses distracts us from considering the obligations of corporations and the government to provide healthy workplace environments and medical care, for example. Focusing attention on the responsibilities of these entities clarifies the relative resourcelessness of individual pregnant women who should not be held fully and singularly responsible for the lack of addiction services in their communities or the presence of toxins in their workplaces—or for the consequences of these problems. Finally, fetuses may be harmed most when pregnant women are defined as potential or actual violators of fetal rights. The characterization may cause pregnant women who need help to avoid prenatal care providers, health care facilities, and other institutions where they have good reason to expect to be judged and punished instead of provided with services.

What is fetal homicide?

Almost forty states have "fetal homicide" laws that deal with crimes against "unborn children *in utero*." State laws apply various definitions to the protected party; many define a "person" as an unborn child at any stage of development, regardless of viability. Under these laws, with titles such as the Preborn Victims of Violence Act, a defendant who has assaulted or murdered a pregnant woman, harming or murdering the fetus, will be punished for crimes against two lives. In some states, the laws specify that this legislation does not apply to legal abortion. Critics of these laws claim that legislation separating the woman from the fetus creates a "slippery slope" that could facilitate criminalization of abortion. These laws, critics warn, can also justify prosecution of the pregnant woman for various behaviors during her pregnancy.

What is the evidence regarding fetal pain?

The concept of fetal pain had a dramatic impact on repro-ductive politics after the film "The Silent Scream" was released in the early 1980s. Dr. Bernard Nathanson, a former abortion-performing physician, decided to make a film to illus-trate the horrors of abortion after hearing President Ronald Reagan speak to a gathering of religious broadcasters about the "long and agonizing pain" of unborn children while they are being "snuffed out." Dr. Nathanson wanted his film to focus on and generate sympathy for the unborn child, not the unwillingly pregnant woman. In an effort to accomplish this, Nathanson focused on the alleged pain even a twelve-week gestational age fetus suffered in the process of an abortion. The film was first aired on the TV show *Jerry Falwell Live*, and has been a hugely successful mainstay of anti-abortion education since then.

Many obstetricians and others have pointed out that whatever scientists ultimately conclude about fetuses and pain, "The Silent Scream" is effective propaganda but not an adequate or accurate vehicle for education about abortion. In the film, the two-inch-long fetus is magnified massively. Dr. Nathanson, as the commentator within the film, stands next to a TV screen showing an abortion in progress. He inter-prets what the viewer is seeing, while holding in his arms a baby-sized doll to explain the position and movements of the fetus. Both the doll and the magnified fetus suggest, visually, that the twelve-week fetus, which Dr. Nathanson refers to as "the child," is the equivalent of a live baby. Nathanson explains that the fetus is recoiling in pain as the abortion instrument makes contact with it. He says, "We see the child's mouth open in a silent scream."

Neonatologists and other scientists have objected to Nathanson's specific identification of fetal body parts that at twelve weeks cannot be visually differentiated in the way Nathanson indicates, and to the doctor's commentary about the meaning of the fetus's movements. Scientists have also objected to his association of pain with a fetus which, in the first trimester, has yet to develop a brain or the neural pathways that are necessary for perceiving and responding to pain. Nevertheless, the film has been very influential, perhaps primarily because of the emotional impact of its association of abortion and fetal pain. Some viewers have argued that no matter what the scientific accuracy of the film, "The Silent Scream" is valuable because it forces viewers to deal with moral questions raised by abortion. Politically, the film continues to be important to the anti-abortion movement because of the ways it explicitly links the movement to compassion for the fetus and implicitly associates abortion providers with deadly violence.

A generation after the release of "The Silent Scream," many states have enacted laws requiring women seeking abortions after twenty-two weeks, or even earlier, to be provided with specific information, using prescribed language, informing them that a fetus of twenty weeks' gestation "has all the physical structures necessary to experience pain," that the fetus will recoil from pain, and that "unborn children who are 20 weeks gestational age or older who undergo prenatal surgery" are routinely administered anesthesia.

These "informed consent" laws break with tradition, as most informed consent laws generally allow the *physician* to determine what relevant information to impart to the patient. Here legislatures and health departments provide the scripts, and physicians are constrained to deliver them in order to fulfill what the statutes identify as the state's obligation to a woman's "right to know" the facts. In this way, the informed consent laws identify the anti-abortion movement, not reproductive rights, with women's rights.

The laws also challenge the "informed consent" standard articulated in *Planned Parenthood of Southeastern Pennsylvania v. Casey*, which requires all information imparted to be both "truthful and not misleading." After all, the question of fetal pain remains unresolved, a subject of scientific study and debate. Indeed, neonatologists agree that certain anatomical structures must be in place before a fetus can experience pain, and that science has not resolved questions about fetal consciousness or awareness of bodily responses. In addition, experts acknowledge that anesthesia is administered for fetal surgery for a number of reasons independent of questions of fetal pain, including to inhibit fetal movement, to prevent uterine contractions, and to prevent hormonal stress responses.[1]

What is fetal viability?

The meaning of "fetal viability"—the capacity of the fetus to live outside the womb—has changed over time. In the middle of the twentieth century, for example, embryologists and neonatologists were in general agreement that fetal viability was reached after approximately thirty-four weeks' gestational age. Scientists and physicians also agreed that fetal viability was a technical term relevant mostly to decision making during an obstetric emergency, such as cases where continuing a pregnancy might cause damage to a major organ in the woman's body or cause her to die. Over the past seventy years, scientific advances, including fetal medicine, have pushed back the number of gestational weeks typically required for a fetus to be able to live outside the womb, with or without artificial support.

Roe v. Wade defined viability as occurring sometime at the start of the third trimester of pregnancy, between weeks 24 and 28, but indicated that because fetuses develop at different rates, the viability of any given fetus would have to be determined by a physician. Also in *Roe v. Wade*, the court ruled that states could not outlaw an abortion after viability if the woman's health or life were at stake. Subsequent to *Roe v. Wade*, the Supreme Court ruled several times—*Missouri v. Danforth*

(1976) and *Colautti V. Franklin* (1979)—that viability is variable and must be determined by the attending physician. Clearly, with these cases and the anti-abortion responses they evoked, "fetal viability" became more than a medical or technical term; now it is also a question of legal status and a political issue.

Abortion after fetal viability has always been very rare in the United States and is almost always sought after the discovery of a catastrophic fetal anomaly or a genetic disorder that guarantees death or profound disability if the pregnancy were to continue to term. In more rare instances, some women seek abortions after fetal viability because of their own severe medical illnesses or psychiatric indications. Nonetheless, most states have passed laws that prohibit abortions at fetal viability, in the third trimester, or most specifically, after twenty-four weeks, the point at which more than 50 percent of fetuses can survive. Recently, states have been considering legislation prohibiting abortion from several weeks to several months before viability.

15

FAMILY BUILDING, REPRODUCTIVE TECHNOLOGIES, AND STEM CELL RESEARCH

What qualifies as a family today?

Traditionally, state governments and religious institutions made laws and rules about marriage and family that were obeyed by almost all Americans who were allowed to marry: a family consisted of a married man and woman and, in time, their children. In the antebellum South, enslaved persons were forbidden by law to marry. For a century afterward, many states enforced laws against marriage by persons of different races, and up to the present, most states forbid the marriage of two persons of the same sex. These laws have enforced normative ideas and rules about who has the capacity and the right to form a family, and they reflect ideas about "family" as a race and gendered privilege.

By the mid-twentieth century, a family that began in the traditional pattern but changed shape, usually because of death or divorce, could still be recognized as a family, albeit a "broken" one. However, individuals, especially women, who formed intimate, domestic relationships in violation of these rules, and those who had children without marriage first, were tagged variously over time as fallen, illegitimate, deviant, criminal, and defiant. Into the late twentieth century, state and religious institutions attempted to deal with the "criminal," the "deviant," and the "defiant" using a variety of strategies, from supporting policies and practices that shunned, silenced, and punished persons in homosexual relationships; to sending white unwed mothers to maternity homes and requiring that their babies be adopted out; to forcing poor mothers to cease their intimate relations to continue to receive public assistance, regardless of whether their sexual partner was the father of their children and their husband.

Many state governments and religious institutions continue to mandate the traditional family pattern. In fact, about thirty states have enacted constitutional bans restricting marriage to one man and one woman; a number of states have simply banned gay marriage. Meanwhile, most Americans continue to form traditional families, although the ratio of Americans living in traditional households—a mother, a father and a child or children—has declined to one in five households according to the 2010 census. In addition, about 40 percent of children are born to unmarried parents now, and over 12 million people are living in unmarried, domestic partnerships, including about 600,000 who are living in households with same-sex partners. More than 39 percent of these same-sex couples, aged twenty-two to fifty-five, are raising children, a figure that represents more than 250,000 children under the age of eighteen.[1] Clearly, increasing numbers of Americans are creating domestic and familial relations that violate prescriptive norms and challenge state laws and religious prescription. In the process, they are redefining the meanings of "marriage" and "family" in ways that place the circumstances of their lives and their own judgments above the traditional mandates of church and state.

For many, the new family forms depend in part on what some have called "the new reproductive logic," in which sex can occur without reproduction (e.g., using contraception or between same-sex couples) and reproduction can occur without sex (via assisted reproductive technologies, or ART). Within this logic, employing ART, lesbian, gay, bi-sexual, transgender, queer, and intersex (LGBTQI) persons—as well as infertile, heterosexual couples—can form genetically related families.

What causes infertility?

Medical experts estimate that about 12 percent of women aged fifteen to forty-four have "impaired fecundity," that is, a diminished capacity to become pregnant; and about 5 percent of men are infertile. Among married women, the estimated rate of infertility is about 7.5 percent, and about 15 percent of married couples face fertility issues.[2]

The causes of infertility include genetic and environmental factors, and endocrine or immune system disorders. Fertility experts indicate that the most frequent cause of infertility is aging, a problem relevant to the fertility of both men and women. (Common estimates are that about one-third of infertility problems are due to male factors and about one-third due to female factors; the source of the rest is unknown.)

Approximately 40 percent of female infertility is associated with problems involving ovulation and the same percentage is associated with problems involving the fallopian tubes. Endometriosis, sexually transmitted diseases, and environmental toxins have all been identified as causes of infertility as well. Some women whose mothers took DES (Diethylstibestrol), a synthetic nonsteroidal estrogen developed in the 1930s and administered to pregnant women from about 1940 to 1971 on the mistaken assumption it would reduce the risk of pregnancy complications and miscarriage, have experienced higher than usual incidences of infertility.

Poor women experience a disproportionately high rate of infertility, because they typically have less access to health care and health education. As a result, this group is more likely to contract sexually transmitted diseases and less likely to obtain medical care for their condition. Also, because of the concentration of hazardous waste sites in poor neighborhoods, both men and women in this category have higher-than-average exposure to industrial, occupational, and environmental toxins, all prime causes of infertility.

Some advocates believe that society should address infertility problems by providing all persons with impaired fecundity who want to become pregnant with comprehensive insurance coverage for appropriate medical treatment, including assisted reproductive technologies. Others believe that while medical coverage is indeed helpful to individuals, relying on insurance and technologies as remedies masks the fact that infertility is the result of larger social problems such as unreasonable workplace pressures that push women to delay childbearing; untreated STDs; and unhealthy workplace conditions. Paying attention to these matters, they claim, would reduce infertility across the board.

What does "assisted reproductive technologies" (ART) refer to?

The development of ART, together with legitimating social and political movements in recent decades, has enabled many people who would not have previously achieved parenthood to do so. For example, assisted reproductive technologies enable single women and men, infertile women and men, LGBTQI persons, and others in reproductively challenging situations to form genetically or nongenetically related families.

In this context, a completely new raft of moral and political questions about reproduction and family has arisen. In fact, some experts and observers have claimed that new reproductive technologies have redefined the concept of "reproductive rights." For example, is the right to reproduce a fundamental human right, and if so, does every person who wants to reproduce have a right to ART and insurance benefits to cover the costs? Is the desire or need to overcome infertility a "socially constructed" matter, as many insurance companies claim, or a valid response to a medical condition, as Europeans generally conclude? With growing public acceptance of single motherhood and gay parenting, is it right for fertility clinics to provide services only to heterosexual couples? What other ethical questions do ART and its adjunct, genetic testing, raise? How does ART shape the way we define not only "family" but key constituent elements: parenthood and kinship itself? For example, must we—and how can we—confront the problem of apportioning parental rights in an extreme case, where one woman donates an egg; another, as "surrogate mother," carries the pregnancy; and a third woman raises the child?

The three most common ways that ART is used to promote pregnancy are alternative insemination (AI); prescription fertility-enhancing drugs; and in vitro fertilization (IVF). Alternative insemination (often referred to as artificial insemination) involves inserting sperm into a woman's body. Sometimes the physician will combine AI with hormonal drugs to stimulate production of multiple eggs, increasing the chances for one of the eggs to be fertilized. The cost of the procedure can vary, depending on whether the sperm is "washed" (a method for separating the sperm from the semen and eliminating any substances that may impair fertilization); whether the sperm is donated or purchased; whether the sperm is inserted into the vagina, the cervix, the uterus, or the fallopian tubes; and whether drugs, ultrasound, and other medical procedures are employed.

Women who do not ovulate or do not ovulate regularly might typically use fertility-enhancing drugs that stimulate production of one or more mature eggs. A woman might use the drug in combination with intercourse, AI, or IVF, or employ the drug regimen on its own.

In vitro fertilization is the method a woman may turn to when other strategies have not led to pregnancy; it is also the most invasive and expensive of the three methods. Using IVF, a woman takes drugs that stimulate her ovaries to produce multiple eggs that are then surgically "retrieved." A woman who does not ovulate can use a donated egg. The egg is then fertilized in a Petri dish and implanted inside the woman's body. In order to achieve a pregnancy, most women using this method go through more than one IVF cycle. Success rates depend on many factors including the reasons for infertility and the age of the woman.

Some people may need either the eggs or sperm of others to achieve pregnancy on their own or via ART. They may purchase gamete material from an egg brokerage agency or a sperm bank; some rely on receiving these materials from a friend or family member. Some men and women have frozen their sperm and eggs, a process called cryopreservation, for use at a later date. Women undergoing chemotherapy have used this method to preserve their reproductive options. Vitrification, a newer technique, freezes eggs so quickly that they are unlikely to form ice crystals, a problem with freezing eggs in the past.

Researchers, practitioners, patients, and others in the ART domain are working in a constantly developing field with many unresolved health and ethical issues. Medical experts and others point out, for example, that the long-term risks of stimulating ovaries to produce multiple eggs have been understudied. Also, during IVF, women are given a drug called Lupron to shut down their ovaries for a time, allowing the physician to control the timing of ovulation. Women report experiencing long-term side effects from taking Lupron, and again, these phenomena are understudied. Women who become pregnant via ART are also much more likely to have multiple gestation pregnancies and multiple births, both of which carry elevated risk for adverse health impacts for women and babies.

Some observers and participants in the ART domain worry about the consequences of the highly commercialized environment in which technology-assisted reproduction is taking place. Fertility clinics market their services in a competitive environment, while young women, looking for income, are undergoing hormonal treatments to sell their eggs for vast sums of money. Sperm banks are marketing sites, too. Some Americans who can afford to are pursuing "reproductive tourism," traveling to countries with lower-cost ART services than they can obtain in the United States, and less restrictive laws. Those seeking services outside the United States might include LGBTQI individuals and couples who are excluded from services by some fertility clinics that serve only heterosexual couples.

Currently there is little state or federal regulation of ART; some experts claim that religious groups and others who oppose assisted reproduction are actively discouraging government regulation of practices they reject. One of the only laws currently regulating ART is the Fertility Clinic Success Rate and Certification Act of 1992. This law requires that fertility clinics report their success rates each year to the Society for Assisted Reproductive Technology (SART). A clinic that fails to report suffers no penalties, although it must be listed on the SART website as nonresponsive. Unfortunately, some women suffer because of this law. The reporting requirement encourages some staff physicians to improve success rates by implanting several embryos at the same time, a tactic that increases multiple births and raises the risk of poor health outcomes for both the woman and the children.

Insurance coverage for ART reflects reproductive politics generally in the United States. For example, no state covers ART for recipients of public assistance, reflecting a widespread attitude that only persons with sufficient resources should reproduce. Many plans exclude unmarried or same-sex couples from coverage, while some states require insurance companies to cover ART costs only in cases of infertility, which can be a strategy for excluding nonheterosexual persons. The insurance mandates of some states apply only to married couples and require the use of the husband's sperm.

What is genetic testing?

Today, many women planning or trying to become pregnant, as well as women in the early stages of pregnancy, want to find out as much as they can about the genetic material and the fetus that will become their child. Women in their thirties and forties, and women with family histories of genetic-related issues, are routinely expected to undergo various kinds of genetic screening. Testing can determine before pregnancy whether there is a genetic mutation present by assessing eggs fertilized in vitro for genetically based problems, before implantation; and assessing the embryo or fetus in utero for genetic anomalies.

Some women undergo testing simply for the information. Others are explicitly interested, or may be interested, in de-selecting a fetus carrying undesirable traits. Women who undergo genetic testing may also participate in genetic counseling to discuss test results. Counseling is intended to help women and their partners understand risks and their consequences and to make informed decisions. Critics of the genetics-testing process point out that the about-to-be pregnant or newly pregnant person cannot become a truly informed, responsible decision maker under these stressful circumstances, yet she is nevertheless pressed to make a quick choice to pursue the pregnancy or not, a particularly pressured decision in states curtailing the period in which legal abortion may occur. Critics also worry about the consequences for parents, children, and society generally of a market-based, testing culture that aims to eliminate variations and "imperfections," and to fulfill the desire of parents for "perfect children."

Why do different groups respond to the idea of genetic testing differently?

Ethicists and others have argued that familiarity with diverse perspectives regarding genetic testing can promote informed public debate and public policies that aim to protect human rights and affirm our shared humanity. These diverse perspectives, some of which are discussed here, also illustrate the challenges embedded in this terrain.

For example, some feminists support genetic testing (sometimes referred to as reprogenetics) because it depends on and updates the idea of "choice" that has been at the heart of struggles for reproductive freedom since *Roe v. Wade*. These proponents might further point out that the constituent elements of "choice"—bodily integrity and decisional autonomy—animate women's decisions today about genetic testing. Other feminists are wary of reprogenetics because of its associations with eugenics and a notion of "choice" that can justify parents' right to "design" their babies. Some feminists do not embrace reprogenetics because of its association with the medicalization of pregnancy and childbearing and with the commercialization of women's bodies and their fertility. Rather than facilitate autonomy and equality, these critics claim, via ART, "reproductive choice" now references "free-market individualism," that is, the right to purchase genetic services and materials. Reproductive rights advocates also worry that a government that regulates reprogenetics may easily enlarge its role in regulating other reproductive options and determining who has the right to access these services.

Some LGBTQI persons and advocates for LGBTQI rights, meanwhile, may support reprogenetics and other reproductive technologies because they facilitate genetically related childbearing *and*, at the same time, facilitate challenges to heteronormativity, even as the new technologies draw clients into normative medicalized, consumerist, family-focused services. Some LGBTQI persons have reported feeling optimistic about the prospect that genetic technologies will discover a "gay gene," giving sexual orientation a scientific basis. Others define the concept of a "gay gene" as simplistic and possibly eugenically dangerous: another trait for de-selection.

Disabled persons and disability rights advocates, again, may celebrate the possibilities and opportunities that repro-genetics provides, but some members of these communities deplore the normalization of de-selection and elimination of potential babies who are not "perfect." They also warn against the practice and the social consequences of defining the genet-ically "flawed" potential child—and for that matter, the dis-abled child and adult—by a trait, and ultimately, simply *as* a trait. Some disability rights advocates argue that normalized de-selection has the effect of further delegitimizing the lives of disabled persons in society and justifying society's disre-gard for the dignity of disabled persons and its lack of atten-tion and allocation of resources to their needs.

Some advocates of racial justice and civil rights have argued that, along with the focus on genetically based health dispari-ties and the development of race-specific medications, genetic testing of embryos, fetuses, and pregnant women amounts to a new form of scientific racism. Within the purviews of these technological developments, "race" is defined as fixed and immutable, raising the possibility for racialized persons to be treated as flawed. Alternately, advocates argue, race can be more accurately defined as a socially constructed concept, constantly in flux, as we see in our everyday lives. Diseases associated with certain racialized groups are not the result of flawed genetic structures, they argue; rather, these health problems generally reflect long- and shorter-term structural inequalities such as environmental and economic impacts, as the emergent scientific field, epigenetics, is suggesting.

What is surrogacy?

Surrogacy occurs when a person who is either unable to pro-duce fertile eggs or who cannot or does not want to carry a pregnancy to term enters into a contractual relationship with a woman who agrees to carry a fertilized egg, give birth to the resulting baby, and usually relinquish any claim to parenthood after birth. The surrogate mother may be paid a fee plus expenses, or she may be paid only for the expenses of pregnancy and delivery. The surrogate may become pregnant when, through artificial insemination, her own egg is fertilized, or via IVF, where the other woman's egg is implanted into the surrogate's uterus. The use of artificial insemination is a far less expensive method. If the surrogate's own egg is used, the procedure is called "traditional surrogacy." A woman who signs a surrogacy contract agreeing to have an in-vitro-fertilized egg of another woman implanted in her uterus is entering into a "gestational surrogacy" contract. In gestational surrogacy, the egg and sperm may come from the intended parents, from donors, or a combination thereof.

Experts agree that the practice of surrogacy is growing rapidly, although there are few reliable statistics tracking the phenomenon, particularly when it comes to measuring the incidence of artificial insemination surrogacy. There is also scant information both about the demographic characteristics of women who enter into surrogacy arrangements and about the physical and mental health effects on these women. Anecdotal evidence suggests that disproportionate numbers of women who contract to carry a pregnancy for another person may be driven by the need to make money; in fact, the explosion of surrogacy arrangements between infertile women in rich countries and fertile women in poor countries such as India suggests that surrogacy is an arena that may ultimately depend on a population of poor women who sell their reproductive capacity to meet their basic needs.

State laws regulating surrogacy are various. Some states hold surrogacy contracts valid and enforceable. Other states prohibit such contracts and punish violators. The laws of most states fall between these two positions. Critics claim that despite the recent increases in the incidence of surrogacy, insufficient regulations governing the practice and the lack of good research, together with the patchwork of state laws, create possibilities for undue risks, exploitation, and confusion.

What ethical questions regarding assisted reproductive technologies remain unresolved?

Unquestionably, ART has enabled hundreds of thousands of fertility-challenged persons to give birth to genetically related babies and has facilitated the births of thousands of healthy babies. Still, these relatively new technologies continue to raise ethical questions. Many questions about the ethical implications of reproductive technologies intersect with questions about reproductive rights, choice, and unborn children. Persons opposing abortion rights are likely to oppose genetic testing as a potential prelude for "de-selection" of an embryo, or because ART may involve the fertilization of multiple ova and the implantation of multiple embryos, some of which may be discarded or aborted in the processes of selecting the most viable genetic material and reducing the number of gestational embryos. One question that arises is how fertility-challenged persons who oppose abortion and believe that life begins at conception square these beliefs with their desire to have a genetically related child, possibly using ART? Additionally, ART takes the issue of fetal rights into new territory; after in vitro fertilization, do the "leftover" embryos have rights? Who decides?

Some observers have argued that the 2011 Arizona law banning abortion after genetic testing for the purpose of sex- or race-selection is fundamentally anti-abortion legislation because it is meant to link abortion to female infanticide and racism, and in the process, bolster the pro-life cause. Whether or not this is true, we may ask if pregnant women are actually using abortion for race- and sex-selection. If so, is this ethical? If not, is it ethical to pass laws outlawing a kind of selection that hardly ever occurs? The law seems to suggest that selective abortion in order to ensure a baby of a preferred sex is more unethical than abortion to de-select for various other traits. Is this so?

ART also intersects with the issue of choice by raising this question: is there a difference (and if so, what difference) between invoking "choice" to justify decisions about whether and when to have a child, and using "choice" to explain the right to create a child with certain, specified traits and not others?

A second arena of ethical dilemmas involves how new technologies make reproduction itself an intensely market-driven activity in both ordinary and entirely new ways. For example, human embryo stem cell research depends on "excess" human eggs produced and collected but no longer needed for ART procedures. Both domains—human stem cell research and ART—transform human tissue into "capital" by normalizing the sale, ownership, and control of the human material of others. These practices use humans as a source of raw material for human-tissue-based industries while at the same time aiming to address and solve major medical problems. This society has yet to confront and legislate matters associated with human cloning; still, the collection, sale, and transfer of human tissue, for whatever reasons, takes us to insufficiently charted ethical frontiers, even as these practices are already in widespread use.

We might also consider payment: sperm donors, egg donors, and surrogate mothers get paid to facilitate the reproductive activity of others. Even our use of the term "donor" in this arena suggests uncertainty about the practice of paying for this kind of assistance. Indeed, when society allows the pregnancy surrogate to be paid, are we encouraging pregnancy-for-profit? Are we recognizing and approving situations in which some women who need money must use their bodies to make a living? Or does this payment represent something else?

Some analysts have called ART the practice of "stratified reproduction," suggesting a third area of ethical uncertainty.

Since ART is the basis of a new reproductive industry, we must ask, what does it take to enter the marketplace where the products of this industry are sold? A number of ethical issues are raised when, under a variety of circumstances, parenthood becomes a class privilege, reserved for individuals and couples who can, in the case of fertility challenges, afford to pay for services. Is it ethically sound to limit parenthood in this and other situations to persons who are economically equipped to reproduce and willing to spend whatever it takes to achieve this goal? There are also unanswered questions regarding the agencies and mechanisms for making decisions in these matters. For example, who decides how much money constitutes "enough" for a woman to legitimately reproduce, or to attempt reproduction with ART?

A fourth area of concern raises ethical questions about individual responsibility versus broader social responsibility, including government participation in providing for health and welfare in the United States. Regarding ART, these issues arise because the promotion of assisted reproductive technologies is consistent with the idea that individuals alone are responsible for problems and remedies regarding fertility challenges and the genetic fitness of their own children. In this way, ART is also consistent with welfare policies that press poor women not to reproduce. In these arenas, public attitudes and public policies promote individual, biological explanations and individual, biologically based solutions for social problems, while eschewing structural explanations (such as high unemployment rates and racism) for social ills and rejecting government responsibility for remedies.

In the case of ART, women and their partners are expected to take full responsibility for making a range of reproductive decisions, including de-selection of fetuses carrying undesirable traits, in order to promote a healthy society. According to some critics, the logic of ART dictates that when the wrong reproductive decisions are made, society suffers. In this formulation, the government and the general society are not responsible for causing or responding to problems such as environmental origins of infertility, nor are they responsible for providing resources to care for disabled babies. Rather, the private, paying citizen—the reproducing woman, in this case—is the source of and the remedy for all such problems.

Finally, ethical problems arise due to the largely unregulated nature of the assisted technology industry. What are the consequences when society asks only that the ART industry recognize "individual rights," defined by safety, qualified insurance coverage, and accessible, accurate information for the consumer? Ethicists and others have called for reproduction- and ART-related goals that go beyond the individual-rights model that drives proponents of "choice" in both the reproductive rights and the ART domains. Some of these goals are recognition of the right to reproduce as a fundamental human right; prevention of eugenic outcomes; opposition of policies that devalue persons with disabilities; equal access to reproductive technologies for people with disabilities, LGBTQI persons, and low-income persons, and support of policies that affirm the right of people in these categories to form families; and allocation of resources to address the environmental causes of infertility and the disproportionate rates of infertility among women of color.

What is the connection between stem cell research and reproductive politics?

Stem cell research is engaged with finding cures for chronic and debilitating conditions such as Alzheimer's disease, Parkinson's disease, spinal cord injuries, juvenile diabetes, and others. The research depends on harvesting special cells from three- to five-day-old embryos donated by fertility clinics; these are often referred to as "surplus embryos" because they are left over after a clinic has conducted fertility treatments. Embryonic stem cells make this research possible because they have the unique ability to develop into more than 200 different cell types in the human body; they are also easier to grow in a laboratory than adult stem cells.

Proponents of stem cell research focus on the "surplus" definition of the genetic material; the embryos that are not used for research are simply discarded. Surely, this group argues, using the embryos to develop life-saving and life-enhancing medicine justifies and even ennobles the practice. Opponents of stem cell research, especially those who believe that life begins at conception, believe that the same moral questions define both this domain and abortion. Opponents argue that stem cell research, like abortion, amounts to homicide, so no degree of good resulting from the research is justifiable. Nationally, Americans are trending toward greater support for stem cell research. Debates about stem cell research and stem cell-based solutions to disease often focus on whether taxpayer money should be used to pay for a practice that is strongly opposed by some Americans. This debate is ongoing, although in the spring of 2011, overturning a 2010 decision blocking public funding, a federal appeals court ruled that taxpayer dollars can be used to fund embryonic stem cell research.

16

ADOPTION

What does adoption look like in the United States today?

In the middle of the twentieth century, adoption became a widespread practice in the United States when thousands of parents and community authorities each year put harsh pressure on shamed, white unmarried girls and women to relinquish their "illegitimate" babies in secret. Almost all adopters then were white, married, infertile couples. Today the situation has changed almost entirely.

Since the early 1970s, in the context of the women's rights movement, women have accrued many rights regarding their fertility. The Supreme Court decision legalizing the right of unmarried persons to possess and use birth control (*Eisenstadt v. Baird*, 405 U.S. 438 [1972]) was a key step, as was the legalization of abortion in 1973. These developments, together with women's access to new educational, economic, and employment opportunities, and the reduced stigma of single motherhood, provided unmarried white females a great deal more latitude to resist the adoption mandate and gave all girls and women more power to decide for themselves how to respond if they became unintentionally pregnant.

A very small number of women of color have relinquished children to nonrelative adopters in the past or the present; today, as mentioned earlier, far fewer white women than in the past relinquish their infants for adoption. There are few demographic data available to help explain the characteristics of the ones who do, but what is known suggests that as a group, relinquishers today are typically in their twenties, often have completed high school, and may have had prior children; they believe they do not have the resources to care for another child. Many of these women come from families and communities in which opposition to abortion is common and from impoverished rural and urban communities. As a group, they have constrained opportunities for educational and employment attainments. Like those who gave up their children in the past, but for different reasons, today's birth mothers constitute an especially vulnerable and resourceless group.

In the current adoption market, the US-born infant is rare. There are few reliable statistics showing how many American infants are adopted, but some experts have estimated the number to be about 14,000 per year, or about one-sixth of US adoptees. This number constitutes about one-third of 1 percent of the more than 4 million babies born a year in the United States.[1]

Infant adoptions in the 1940s to the 1970s were shrouded in secret, ostensibly to protect the reputation and future marriageability of unwed white females who had given birth and their families. Today, domestic infant adoptions are likely to be "open," with relinquishing women choosing adopters from among sets of detailed information and photographs. Adopters frequently attend the birth of the child they are to adopt, and channels of continuing communication often are kept open between the birth mother and the adopter for varying periods.

Most children who are adopted by people other than their stepparents (these adoptions account for about 40 percent of total adoptions) are adopted via child welfare agencies (68 percent). Of all children whose adoptions are facilitated by these agencies, which charge only a nominal fee for adoption services, more than half are adopted by the adults who were already the child's foster parents (54 percent) or by relatives (32 percent). To keep these figures in perspective, it is important to know that among all children exiting foster care in a given year, only about 20 percent are adopted. In addition, among the more than 400,000 children in foster care in a given year, over 100,000 are waiting for placement in adoptive homes.[2]

In any given year, about half of all children in foster care are reunified with their families. The only foster children who are available for adoption are those whose parents have had their parental rights terminated by the state under charges of "abuse and neglect," a charge that is disproportionately brought against poor black women. A number of scholars and public policy experts, using cross-class data about parental behaviors and other variables, assess this policing practice as racist.[3]

About 15 percent of adopted children, or slightly fewer than 13,000, are adopted from other countries each year. Just under one-quarter of these children come from China, followed by children from Ethiopia (17 percent), Russia (12 percent), South Korea (8.6 percent), Guatemala (6 percent), and Ukraine (5 percent), among more than forty countries. For some years, until recently, Guatemala had sent the largest number of children per year, up to four thousand. In 2008, Guatemala began work to bring its adoption practices into compliance with the Hague Convention on the Protection of Children and Cooperation in Respect of Inter-Country Adoption, so the number of children adopted from Guatemala has declined dramatically. China, too, has tightened its regulations and requirements in recent years.[4]

Who adopts infants and foreign-born children in the United States?

Adopters before the 1970s were almost always white, middle-class, heterosexual couples who could meet agencies' stringent economic and home-study standards. Today, many adoption agencies have more flexible policies regarding sexual orientation, race, and "race matching" of the adopters and the child; however, the costs of some adoption strategies may continue to limit infant adoption to people with access to substantial resources.

Through various agencies and some post-foster-care opportunities, single persons and LGBTQI persons can adopt. Most mainstream legal, medical, and social service organizations that deal with adoption have issued statements supporting adoption by gays and lesbians. Still, some of the biggest sources of adoptable children, such as China and Ethiopia, exclude "homosexuals." Chinese agencies may place children with married couples through their premium adoption programs, while offering older or "less desirable" children to unmarried adopters, who may be asked to verify that they are single and "non-homosexual." With the high costs of infant adoption and inter-country adoption ($5,000 to more than $40,000, depending on services and other factors), few lower-income individuals and couples can afford to adopt children in these categories.

National statistics show that one-half of women who adopt a child are between forty and forty-four years old, and only 3 percent are under thirty. Most people who adopt are heterosexual, married couples (including most of the 40 percent of adopters who are the child's stepparent), but the number of single men and women who adopt has been increasing steadily in recent years, reflecting the overall growth in single-person-headed households with children. Not surprisingly, women who have used infertility services without success are ten times more likely to have adopted children than women who have never used these services.[5]

Why is inter-country adoption controversial?

Some observers of inter-country or "foreign" adoption have noted that this practice, which boomed after women in the United States gained reproductive rights and white women virtually stopped relinquishing their babies for adoption, depends on women in poor countries providing babies for women in rich countries. They have also noted that inter-country adoption generally takes place after protracted wars with the United States (Korea, Vietnam); in the wake of repressive state action against indigenous people's movements (Guatemala); following enactment of national population policies (China); and other forms of social upheaval and privation that undermine the safety of women and children. Thus, these observers note, the American woman's "choice" to adopt depends on the "choicelessness" of the poorest and most resourceless women around the world. These critics also point out that a high incidence of adoption in a country or geographical region is an accurate index of the low status of women in that location. Critics observe that in their eagerness to find a child to call their own, persons wishing to adopt babies often efface the interests of the relinquishing mother, including what some, such as legal scholar Dorothy Roberts, have called a woman's human right to be a mother.[6]

Proponents of inter-country adoption say that white Americans who adopt children of color are promoting racial tolerance within families and communities in the United States, but critics question whether this is so, arguing instead that the practice justifies and exemplifies the power of wealthy, white Americans to become parents by treating the reproductive bodies of poor women and their children, who are often poor people of color, as "natural resources" available for purchase as mere commodities. The critics maintain that inter-country adoption thus promotes attitudes of racial superiority and racial privilege in the United States.

On the other hand, advocates of inter-country adoption have pointed out that transferring children from poor countries to rich ones facilitates family building for people profoundly committed to parenthood. Equally important, they say, this activity is clearly a form of child rescue, a perspective that has supported the extra-legal removal of hundreds of children from their families in Haiti and other disaster zones. Indeed, advocates explain that adoption provides a way to remove children from environments characterized by dire poverty and privation and provide them with a strong family, education, and prospects—a good life—in the United States. Advocates also argue that relinquishing mothers clearly cannot take care of the children they give up for adoption and that these women desperately want a good life for their children, which is why they are eager to find North Americans and other "rich" people to adopt them. Furthermore, they contend, as noted, that creating families across racial differences contributes to a more tolerant society in the United States. And finally, some advocates point out that foreign adoption is practical because it is possible—unlike the United States, China, Ethopia, and other countries do have many babies available for adoption—and it is the "safer" way to go since the faraway birth mother is very unlikely to attempt to reclaim her child should she change her mind after the adoption.

In the early 1990s, human rights advocates, witnessing some of the conditions under which poor mothers around the world were giving up children and weighing in with their concerns about the rights of these women, oversaw the establishment in 1993 of the Hague Convention on Intercountry Adoption. This document favors family preservation over adoption and favors adoption within the child's country over inter-country adoption. It also stresses that every adoption must be in the best interests of the child, and that signatory countries agree to use ethical practices within and between countries; each signatory country secures this commitment by appointing a "central authority" or a system of central authorities within the country to administer and oversee adoption practices. The Hague Convention indicates that mothers who relinquish their children should be exercising *choice*; however, critics have pointed out that "choice" is a difficult matter to define or assess when the mother is living under conditions of material scarcity, political repression, and gender-based discrimination, not uncommon for mothers in countries with high rates of relinquishment. The Hague Convention became active with respect to the United States on April 1, 2008. Most babies from other countries who are adopted by Americans come from nations that are not signatories to the convention.

What laws govern adoption in the United States?

Each state in the United States holds the major responsibility for creating law and policy to govern its own child welfare services, including adoption. Laws and regulations vary from state to state, and each state administers its own legal and administrative structures and programs. However, all states must comply with certain federal requirements regarding adoption in order to be eligible for various kinds of federal funding involving adoption. New federal laws often require federal departments and agencies to issue or amend policies and regulations, and they prompt states to enact legislation, revise the policies and regulations of state agencies, and develop new programs, all in order to comply with federal law. For example, the federal Adam Walsh Child Protection and Safety Act of 2006 requires prospective foster or adoptive parents to have background and fingerprint checks. Also, the Fostering Connections to Success and Increasing Adoptions Act of 2008 doubled the incentive payments for adopting special needs and older children; at the same time, it required these children to be full-time students unless there was a medical condition making this impossible.

17

THE ENVIRONMENT AND REPRODUCTIVE POLITICS

How are environmental contaminants affecting reproductive health in the United States?

No one knows for sure the relationship between contaminants and reproduction, but there are some indications that the effects are felt nationwide. Today, chemical production in the United States is a $450 billion industry, manufacturing and mining products that Americans come into contact with all day long. Chemicals are in the air and the water; in our food, clothes, cosmetics, and pharmaceuticals; in house paint, mattresses, refrigerators, cell phones, household cleaning supplies, building materials, and cars. Some Americans experience very high levels of chemical exposure, particularly if they live near chemical plants, in agricultural areas where pesticides are used, or in heavily air-polluted urban areas. The Toxic Substances Control Act, which was passed by Congress in 1976 and has not been updated despite the development of many new chemicals and uses, does not require manufacturers to prove that their products meet safety standards; consequently, only a very small percentage of the chemicals in circulation have been tested for health impacts. For most chemicals, including hundreds used in consumer products, we have no information about whether they have adverse effects on reproductive functions and human development.[1]

American scientists have been aware for many decades that some chemicals have had specific harmful impacts on human development. In 1962, Dr. Frances Kelsey, a pharmacologist at the Food and Drug Administration, worked hard to remove thalidomide, a tranquilizer prescribed to pregnant women as an anti-nausea agent, from the American market after it was shown to cause deformation of fetal limbs. Kelsey and others understood that thalidomide's impact demonstrated that the fetus can be uniquely sensitive to chemical exposure. As mentioned earlier, in 1971, Diethylstilbestrol, or DES, a synthetic nonsteroidal estrogen that obstetricians had been prescribing to American women to prevent miscarriages, was shown to cause a rare form of cervical and vaginal cancer in the daughters of women who had been given the drug during pregnancy. Over time, research showed that both sons and daughters of these women had high rates of infertility and other reproductive problems. This episode clarified chemical impacts across generations, as even the reproductive functioning of grandchildren was affected.

Today, scientists estimate that the reproductive health of Americans has deteriorated significantly from that of their grandparents, citing developments such as the declining sperm counts many men experience, especially those living in certain industrialized regions of the country, and the rise in the incidence of breast, testicular, and prostate cancers. Reproductive epidemiologists, toxicologists, and other scientists and medical clinicians have developed clear evidence in recent years that chemical exposures are ubiquitous and harmful to reproductive and other functions. A 2011 study of 286 pregnant women detected 43 banned and contemporary chemicals in the bloodstreams of 99 to 100 percent of the women. Other studies have shown that starting at conception, humans are exposed to hundreds of chemicals or more that can cause health problems across their life span. These may include low birth weight, fetal anomalies, learning disabilities, childhood cancers, diabetes, and adult cancers, among other problems.[2]

Scientific research today is linking chemical exposures to increased incidence of compromised reproductive systems among both women and men, and also to the reproductive system as a transmitter of health challenges to subsequent generations. Studies are focusing on relationships between various environmental contaminants before and during pregnancy and specific adverse outcomes, including infertility, compromised fecundity, and high rates of miscarriage; pregnant women's exposure to air pollutants and perinatal outcomes, including infant mortality; exposure to certain plastics during critical periods of fetal development and the incidence of fetal anomalies; persistent exposure to environmental contaminants and the incidence of low sperm quality and high rates of endometriosis; exposure to workplace chemicals and adverse pregnancy outcomes; and male and female exposure to pesticides and synthetic fertilizers and male subfertility, high miscarriage rates, menstruation problems, and other reproductive health problems. Studies are also suggesting connections between early puberty and menopause and environmental or lifestyle conditions. Recent studies in California and New York have shown that children who as fetuses were exposed to substantial levels of neurotoxic pesticides have lower IQs when entering school.

Reproductive health experts who focus on environmental impacts and their consequences warn that some of their findings are unexpected and ominous, and they suggest the need for a great deal more study. For example, findings show that even low doses of or exposure to some contaminants can alter gene expression. Other studies show that human exposure to chemical *mixtures*, which is very common, causes harm to reproductive functions that is more serious than if the exposure is to a single chemical. Finally, scientists have found lifelong effects when the egg or sperm has been exposed, or if the exposure is in utero. But the ability of scientists to predict which groups and individuals are most susceptible to harm from exposure is still underdeveloped. Scientists working in this area generally agree that many factors can contribute to heightened reproductive vulnerability to environmental exposures, including age, gender, genetic and epigenetic variation, diet and obesity, infections, disease history and treatments, lifestyle factors such as drug use, and occupation.

Beyond these factors, scientists, physicians, scholars, and advocates are paying more attention to how socioeconomic and racial disparities and the experience of living or working near certain industries and industrial accidents creates heightened vulnerability for reproductive-related impacts from environmental exposures. Community activists are bringing attention to reproductive health impacts in communities of color and indigenous communities due to contaminated military sites in Alaska and New Mexico; to the operation of medical and solid waste incinerators in East Oakland, California; to the exposure of immigrant nail salon workers to common beauty industry chemicals in unventilated working conditions, and other such situations.

Environmental scientists and others working in this area are focused on basic questions of public health as well as on the right of humans to environmental safety, including freedom from exposure to contaminants that can harm their reproductive capacity and outcomes. They warn that the lack of attention to these matters, the lack of funding to pursue testing and solutions, and the failure to empower official oversight to regulate this arena will have dire consequences for the viability of the population in the future.

What are environmentalists saying about population growth, consumption, and challenges to global sustainability?

Since the publication of Paul and Anne Erlich's book, *The Population Bomb*, in 1968, a number of US environmentalists have identified population expansion as one of the largest problems affecting the country and the planet. Proponents of this view say that while rapid rates of population growth have subsided recently, there are still about 80 million babies born each year, a rate that will bring world population to over 9 billion by 2050. This is simply too many people, they argue, for the earth's resources—water, forest, energy, food—to support. In the past, many population-control organizations supported government-based sterilization and contraception mandates that were unconcerned with women's interests and sought to constrain the fertility rates of poor women in particular.

Today, however, proponents of population reduction support efforts in the United States and around the world to make contraception and sometimes abortion available to women, arguing that 100 million women in the poorest communities and countries want to control their fertility but lack the means to do so. Such organizations today are more likely to talk in terms of women's reproductive rights and the relationship between elevation in the status of women and falling rates of reproduction. They also underscore how the eradication of poverty goes hand-in-hand with reduced fertility rates.

Other environmentalists identify the most profound source of environmental degradation as lavish consumption supported by nonrenewable energy in developed countries. Some proponents of this view say that most population growth in the future will occur among the poorest people on earth, who would still consume the fewest resources and contribute the smallest share of greenhouse gases, while people in the richest countries continue to consume at environmentally disastrous levels.

Many environmentalists reject the either/or nature of this discussion, advocating reduced and more environmentally sensible consumption in rich countries *and* reduced rates of reproduction in all countries in which growth rates exceed standards of sustainability. Still, as answers are sought, governmental officials, scientists, human rights activists, and others have to face what appears to be a terribly paradoxical conundrum as they seek perspectives and solutions: reducing poverty reduces population growth, but increasing wealth is the surest path to increased consumption and resource depletion.

What are the implications of these environmental perspectives for the most vulnerable women?

When state governments began to distribute welfare funds under the Social Security Act of 1935, many states restricted benefits to white mothers only. From the 1940s to the 1970s, the federal government intermittently pressed states to stop using racialized exclusions. Though states complied, they often justified benefits on the bases of racialized environmental crises—overpopulation, crowded cities, crime—and population-control principles, requiring poor mothers of color, in particular, to be celibate, or pressing them to have abortions or to be sterilized or take contraceptives. From this time onward, in the United States and abroad, population policies have often targeted the bodies of the poorest and most vulnerable women. These policies and practices obscure women's health and material needs, while focusing blame for environmental degradation on those with the least means. They also obscure the broader, industrial causes of resource depletion and other environmental problems.

Over the past several decades, the environmental justice movement and activists drawing attention to environmental racism have pointed out that landfills, incinerators, and power plants are almost always built where poor people of color live, causing especially high rates of breast cancer, infertility, miscarriage, and birth anomalies in these communities. Those who draw attention to these matters provide many examples. They cite industrial waste and contamination in the Gulf states causing long-term residents, mostly African

American and Latina/o, to test positive for chemicals linked to infertility, miscarriage, low birth rate, low sperm count, and developmental and respiratory disorders for children exposed in utero. Mohawk and other indigenous peoples have organized to demand remediation of toxic waste sites such as the PCB-filled open lagoons leaking into the St. Lawrence River, a crucial waterway for Mohawks. The toxins are contaminating the Mohawks' food chain, including the milk of lactating mothers. And Latina/o activists are demanding attention to the fact that 66 percent of their population lives in areas of the United States where air quality does not meet EPA standards, a condition of life causing disproportionately negative impacts on pregnant Latina women and their children.[3]

18

DISABILITY AND REPRODUCTIVE POLITICS

What basic reproductive restrictions have been placed on women with disabilities in the past and today?

Historically, the medical community and general society considered disabled women—those who were born with genetic anomalies, or acquired disabilities associated with diseases such as cerebral palsy or polio, or became disabled due to accidents—"unfit" for sexual relations and for motherhood. Disabling traits or characteristics were typically associated with biological degradations and social problems that society believed should not be transmitted. Girls and women with Down syndrome, muscular dystrophy, mental illnesses, and other genetic and nongenetic disabilities were often denied sex education and gynecological health services. Many were institutionalized or otherwise sequestered, and some were sterilized.

Surprisingly, after a generation and more of civil and human rights movements, as well as the rise of the disability rights movement, many in the medical professions and in the population at large still deem disabled persons unsuitable for sexuality and reproduction. In this cultural context, women with disabilities (WWD) often report being discouraged from becoming mothers because their physicians and others say that, as disabled parents unable to care for their children adequately, they would be creating additional burdens for their families and communities—and for their children.

Many women with disabilities report that their health care providers transmit negative attitudes toward the reproductive capacities of WWD by not asking about their sexual lives and neglecting to ask about or assess their reproductive health—for example, by failing to perform full, regular pelvic examinations. In addition, women with disabilities may have poor access to mobility devices, public transportation, medical buildings with handicap accommodations, and health care. They may lack access to computers or have limited contact with other WWD and consequently be unable to acquire the reproductive health information they need. They may be uncomfortable communicating about sexuality and its outcomes, including reproduction, because of stigmas and taboos often affixed to the association of disabled persons and sex. Altogether, women with disabilities report that these attitudes and access issues create a hostile environment in which WWD attempt to define, claim, and enact reproductive rights.

Even given this cultural context, the disability rights movement has been a growing force, objecting to traditional views of the bodies of women with disabilities and their sexual and reproductive possibilities. Through various organizations including the Disability Justice Collective, the disability rights movement has advocated effectively for the reproductive rights of women with disabilities and, in the process, has created perspectives and language that aim to fuel the reproductive rights claims of individual WWD and reshape mainstream thinking about these matters.[1]

How have prenatal diagnostics shaped Americans' view of disability?

In the United States, most women expect the law to protect their ability to make reproductive choices. At the most basic level, they expect to be able to have a choice about whether and when to get pregnant. Many also expect to make a choice within the first trimester of pregnancy about whether or not to stay pregnant. Increasingly, the fertility industry and some medical practitioners, building on the consumerist lingua franca that characterizes this domain, are presenting additional aspects of reproduction as "choices," a development that is having significant impacts on ideas about disabled persons and on the experiences of people in disability communities.[2]

For example, as discussed in Chapter 15, women undergoing IVF and other forms of assisted reproduction go through a process of selection of their "best" embryos to maximize the chances for a good outcome and to avoid what the industry often calls "the devastation" of giving birth to a baby with a genetically based anomaly. When pregnant women undergo ultrasound testing and amniocentesis, they are entering into another process that depends on "choice," this time the process of de-selecting and aborting fetuses carrying genes associated with disabilities such as Down syndrome, spina bifida, sickle cell anemia, and many others. As discussed previously, this new frontier offers the possibility for pregnant women and their partners to make choices for sex selection or to choose other traits and characteristics they value or want to avoid as they "design" their new family member.

All of these processes are presented and can surely be experienced as "individual choices" made with no considerations beyond the preferences of the parents. Yet disability rights activists point out that these choices, like all choices, are made within a social context. In this case, the choices express a high valuation of some kinds of bodies and the devaluation of others which, if they occur, bring disappointment or worse to parents and others. These advocates make the point that participating in some of these processes is now more than just a choice; ultrasound and amniocentesis have become virtual responsibilities for pregnant women beyond their early thirties. Now implicitly, even explicitly, ever-larger percentages of pregnant women and their partners are affirming their immutable preference for a "perfect baby." These developments, according to those concerned with the dignity and human rights of disabled persons, are contributing to the isolation and indignity of disabled children and adults in US society today.

Some proponents of the human rights and reproductive dignity of disabled persons have described a central paradox they face when supporting a woman's right to make reproductive decisions, including the right to have an abortion, while objecting profoundly to the eugenic basis of many of these decisions.[3]

19

BIRTHING, BREAST-FEEDING, AND REPRODUCTIVE POLITICS

In what settings are babies born in the United States today?

In 1900 more than 95 percent of American women gave birth at home. Fourteen years later, anesthesia, or "twilight sleep," was first used to dull labor pains, accelerating over time the transition of birthing from home to hospital. By 1960, today's pattern—almost all women have hospital births attended by physicians—had become the norm. Many women choose hospital births over birthing centers or home births because certain anesthetics are uniquely available in this setting, as is complete emergency equipment.

A large-scale recent study of women in twenty-seven states who had singleton births (one baby) in vaginal deliveries showed that nearly two-thirds had epidural or spinal anesthesia during labor, with non-Hispanic white women, more highly educated women, those who began prenatal care earliest, and those attended by a physician more likely than other groups to use these drugs. The study also showed that older women were less likely to use these particular anesthetics.[1] The American College of Obstetricians and Gynecologists, pointing out that "there are no other circumstances in which it is considered acceptable for an individual to experience severe pain, amenable to safe intervention, while under a doctor's care," recommends that women in labor receive pain relief upon request.

Critics of in-hospital, physician-attended deliveries cite various aspects of the medicalization of birth, including fewer choices for the parturient woman under hospital rules, such as those regarding food, drink, body position, mobility, use of electronic monitoring, intravenous (IV) preparations, and medical induction.

The World Health Organization reports that over 90 percent of births worldwide are classified as "normal," or uncomplicated, a fact that bolsters the decisions of some pregnant women to de-medicalize their birthing process. A very small percentage of total births in the United States occurs in licensed birthing centers, usually attended by midwives or nurses, and occasionally by physicians, with a backup hospital nearby. These low-tech settings usually stress a family-centered, natural childbirth philosophy, inviting the pregnant woman to include her family and others in the experience, and encouraging women to make their own choices about many matters that are regimented in hospitals. Staff usually expect the woman to have received childbirth education, such as Lamaze or Bradley training, and to commit to natural pain management. About 6 percent of women who have had prior babies and 25 percent of first-time mothers transfer from the center to hospitals for delivery, mostly for nonemergency situations.[2] While these facilities are usually less expensive than hospitals, some insurance plans do not cover birthing centers, a situation that has limited access to these settings. The Patient Protection and Affordable Care Act of 2010 includes guaranteed facility fee payments to birth centers.

The economics of pregnancy and giving birth have structured many aspects of the childbearing experience. Birthing options, including access to midwives and birthing centers, have only been available to women with excellent insurance or extensive resources of their own. Undocumented women, immigrants who have been in the United States for fewer than five years and therefore are not eligible for Medicaid, and other uninsured women have been limited to hospital births, whether they want a medicalized experience or not, often under the supervision of a doctor they have never met before. (Most of these women have been eligible for Emergency Medicaid, which covers labor and delivery in the hospital, but not for prenatal care, except in cases of complicated pregnancies.) Women living in rural settings have also generally had few birthing options, especially since so many small hospitals have been closed during periods of fiscal austerity over the past generation, and as health care has been increasingly corporatized and facilities consolidated. From 2014 onward, the Affordable Care Act is scheduled to cover pregnancy and newborn care as "essential health benefits." Also, insurers will no longer be able to exclude a current pregnancy or any feature of delivery (such as a previous cesarean or episiotomy) as a preexisting condition.

What status do midwives have in the United States?

In the middle of the twentieth century, the practice of midwifery—usually by a nurse certified by a nationally accredited program to assist women throughout the childbearing cycle, including in childbirth—began its slow climb back to obstetric respectability after having been de-credentialed through the efforts of the American Medical Association and other regular medical organizations approximately 100 years earlier. In some parts of the United States, chiefly the South within African American communities, midwives had continued to practice to some degree. Generally, however, as birthing moved into hospitals and came almost fully under the authority of medical doctors, midwifery was outlawed in many states and all but died out.

In 1955, Columbia-Presbyterian-Sloan Hospital in New York became the first mainstream medical institution to allow midwives to deliver babies, and five years later the US Children's

Bureau started funding several nurse-midwife education programs. In the 1970s, some participants in the women's movement championed natural childbirth, women-centered birthing practices, and the revival of lay midwifery.

Today most states have legalized midwifery, although nine continue to completely outlaw it. Other states have laws that limit the situations in which midwives can practice. Of midwife-attended births, about 95 percent take place in hospitals (making up approximately 6 pecent to 8 percent of all hospital births), 3 percent in birthing centers, and 1 percent in home settings. Midwives employ practices that aim to obviate the need for medical induction, and births under the supervision of midwives end up with a dramatically lower percentage of caesarean sections (C-sections) than physician-supervised births.

Why is the rate of caesarian section so much higher in the United States than it used to be?

A caesarean delivery is one in which the infant, the placenta, and the membranes are extracted from the woman's body through an incision in her abdominal and uterine walls. Generally, a C-section is performed when, due to dangerous maternal or fetal stress, the delivery must occur at once.

Around 1999, after nearly a decade of stability, the rate of caesarean sections began to rise sharply; today nearly one out of three births is a caesarean delivery. The rates have increased for mothers in all ages and racial groups. They have increased in all states, with some states (Colorado, Connecticut, Florida, Nevada, Rhode Island, and Washington) seeing increases of up to 70 percent. At present, even in the states with the lowest rates (Alaska, Idaho, New Mexico, and Utah) about one in four births is caesarean. In the states with the highest rates (Florida, Louisiana, Mississippi, New Jersey, and West Virginia), over one in three births is caesarean, in some hospitals as high as four or five out of ten. The World Health Organization has stated that the cesarean rate for any region should not exceed 10 percent to 15 percent.[3]

Public health experts and other researchers and observers have suggested a number of reasons for increased reliance on this surgery today; many are nonmedical reasons. These include physician practice patterns, that is, a desire to fit births into the hours of the physician's work schedule; insufficient hospital staffing; more conservative practice guidelines, such as lowering the number of permissible hours of labor before intervention; and financial and legal pressures, including physicians' beliefs that surgical intervention is more likely to guarantee a positive outcome and avoidance of malpractice actions. Other possible reasons include more older women giving birth (although rates have increased among all maternal ages); more multiple births today (and caesarean rates are high for this group, although the rates for singleton births have increased substantially more than for multiples); and more women choosing for various reasons to give birth by caesarean.

In addition, studies show that the practice of inducing labor is closely related to incidence of caesareans. About 44 percent of women in a large study who attempted to deliver vaginally were induced (administered a drug to speed up and intensify their labor, shortening the period before delivery). Members of this group were two times more likely to deliver by caesarean section than women who went into labor on their own. Other studies have reported a rate of induced labor of about one in five, which is approximately twice the 1990 rate.[4]

In the mid-1990s, 30 percent of women who had delivered by C-section went on to give birth vaginally. Approximately twenty years later, about 10 percent of women who have previously had caesarean sections are having subsequent deliveries vaginally, perhaps because success rates for VBACs (vaginal birth after caesarean) have been reported between only 60 percent and 80 percent. Still, prominent analysts have argued that the reduced rate of VBACs is conditioned by nonmedical factors such as physicians' pressures on parturient women to have subsequent C-sections, despite the dangers associated with multiple caesareans.[5] As some causes of high caesarean rates appear to be nonclinical, the rapid-rate increases suggest that pregnant women themselves may not be well informed about the risks associated with caesarean sections, or may be giving birth in facilities that do not adequately follow (or loosely define) informed consent procedures. These risks include higher rates of surgical complications and maternal rehospitalization following this major abdominal surgery; higher rates of neonatal admission to intensive care when mothers encounter complications; and high costs and longer recuperations associated with caesarean sections.

What is natural childbirth?

In 1944, Grantly Dick-Read, the British obstetrician who had promoted nonmedicalized birthing for some years, published his groundbreaking book, *Childbirth without Fear: The Principles and Practices of Natural Childbirth,* in the United States. The book appeared only a few years after anesthesia became standard practice in obstetric medicine and at about the time that three-quarters of all American women living in cities gave birth at hospitals rather than at home as they had before.

Dick-Read, responding to such developments, wanted to remind women of the success of earlier, natural (nonmedicalized) birth practices and alert them to the risks and degradations, as he saw it, that attended many hospital deliveries. As founder of the natural childbirth movement, he aimed to educate modern women about the superior experience of giving birth with as limited a degree of medical intervention as possible. Dick-Read was a champion of women entering into the birthing experience fully educated about what to expect, possessing breathing strategies and other self-directed tactics for dealing with labor and delivery pain. He advocated the commitment by parturient women to a drug- and implement-free process, if possible. Dick-Read believed that pain was a by-product of the fear women had been trained to associate with childbirth. Proper preparation, he claimed, could dissipate fear and put women in charge of their birth experiences. Dick-Read and his popular successors such as Dr. Fernand Lamaze, have stressed that parturient women, bolstered by the confidence that follows this kind of preparation, can transcend pain, be more likely to have uncomplicated deliveries, and produce healthier babies.

Is there a maternal health care crisis in the United States?

Even though the United States spends more money on pregnancy and childbirth-related hospital services than any other country, every day two to three women die during pregnancy and childbirth in this country. Women in forty other countries have a smaller lifetime risk than American women of dying from pregnancy-related complications. For example, a woman in the United States is five times more likely to die in childbirth than a woman in Greece and four times more likely than a woman in Germany. Maternal health services are not equally accessible in the United States to all women: those living in low-income areas of the country are twice as likely to die during or very soon after their pregnancies as women living in high-income areas. According to a recent study of maternal health in the United States by Amnesty International, high maternal death rates have stemmed in part from the fact that 13 million women of childbearing age have no health insurance, a situation that should be ameliorated by the Affordable Care Act. Up to this point, however, women of color have comprised about one-third of the reproductive-age female population and over one-half of all uninsured women. About one in three pregnant African American and Native American women have not received adequate prenatal care beginning in the first trimester, and Medicaid-eligible women have often encountered delays when they try to access medical services. In addition, the study reports that 64 million Americans live in "shortage areas," rural and urban locations in which there are not enough medical personnel to serve the population's need for primary medical care, including maternal care. Many women living in these areas lack transportation to get to prenatal clinics, have jobs that don't allow them time off for doctors' appointments, and lack child care. The Amnesty International study reports that a majority of the maternal deaths in the United States and many pregnancy-related complications would be preventable if all pregnant women received adequate health care.[6]

What do medical authorities say about the relationship between breast-feeding and infant health?

The World Health Organization has recommended that infants be breast-fed exclusively for the first six months of life, and in 2011 the US Surgeon General Regina M. Benjamin issued a "Call to Action to Support Breastfeeding," urging communities, employers, and health care systems to promote and facilitate breast-feeding. The call cited evidence that breast-feeding protects babies from infections and illnesses that include diarrhea, ear infections and pneumonia, asthma, and obesity, and that it decreases the risk for breast and ovarian cancers among mothers who nurse.

Some studies have associated breast-feeding with environmental health risks because various dangerous toxins in plastics, paint thinners, termite poisons, flame retardants, dry-cleaning fluids, and other common products end up in breast milk. Recent studies, however, have found that the toxic load in breast milk is less dangerous than the typical American infant's exposure to airborne pollutants and does not significantly compromise the health benefits of nursing.[7]

Without question, many new mothers—those whose employers provide no paid maternity leave and those eligible for some limited paid leave—are unable to provide their infants with an exclusive diet of breast milk, even with extensive pumping. Some public health experts and other advocates of breast-feeding have noted that because the United States does not have a national paid maternity leave policy, breast-feeding as a route to infant health has become a privilege fully available only to babies whose mothers can afford to stay home during the early months.

Must employers allow employees to express milk with breast-pumps while at work?

After the passage of the Patient Protection and Affordable Care Act in 2010, the Fair Labor Standards Act of 1938 was amended to require an employer to provide reasonable break time for an employee to express breast milk as often as she needs to for her nursing child for up to one year after giving birth. The employer is not required to compensate the employee for this time but must provide a place, other than a bathroom, that can be used for this purpose. An employer with fewer than fifty employees who can show that providing these accommodations causes hardship to the business, can be exempted from these requirements.

Do states have laws about breast-feeding in public?

Forty-four states have laws that specifically allow women to breast-feed in any public or private location; about two-thirds of these exempt breast-feeding from "public indecency" laws. About a dozen states exempt breast-feeding women from jury duty, and a small number of states have launched educational programs about the benefits of breast-feeding.

20

MEN AND REPRODUCTIVE POLITICS

In what ways are reproductive rights the concerns of men as well as women?

With the ongoing rise in single pregnancy and motherhood, and continuing patterns of disproportionate maternal responsibility for child rearing, men are typically less connected to and less likely to take responsibility for the health and safety of fetuses and children. The cultural ideas about masculinity that facilitate many men's distance from reproductive and family matters impose burdens on both men and women, including the costs of eliding and neglecting the status of male reproductive health and dignity.

Reproductive health studies indicate that the rise of male reproductive-related health problems—decreased semen viability, sexually transmitted diseases, and increased rates of testicular cancer, for example—makes clear that bacterial, viral, and other environmental threats are having harmful impacts on the reproductive bodies of both women and men as well as on fetuses and children. Another issue men face is that as reproductive materials (ova and sperm) are in high demand, the marketplace increasingly commodifies these human products while challenging concepts of human beings—both women and men—that resist commodification. In addition, sperm banks select donors using eugenically inflected criteria, and women purchasing sperm are often expected to choose batches based on this same kind of donor information. Sperm classification mirrors the ads featuring ova from the bodies of beautiful, young, white women at Ivy League universities. Many men, just like many women, are experiencing health threats, commodification, and race and class bias centered on their reproductive bodies.

Beyond these common experiences, some men define reproductive rights or reproductive justice as their issue as well because these arenas depend on the core claim that a woman has the right to manage her own body, including the right to decide whether or not and when to be a mother, and the right to access the resources she requires to do this with safety and dignity. Proponents, both men and women, identify these ideas as human rights claims, key to human autonomy and an anti-racist, anti-sexist culture that opposes oppression in all its forms.

On a personal level, many men, recognizing that reproductive issues have a much more direct and profound impact on the lives of women than men, demonstrate their identification with reproductive rights by taking responsibility for their own reproductive health and fertility control, and by supporting community-based institutions and resources to provide this care for their partners and others.

Has the so-called men's rights movement influenced discussion about men's roles in reproductive decision making?

In the decades following the rise and public policy successes of the feminist movement in the 1960s and 1970s, a loosely organized backlash movement emerged made up of men who believed that feminism harmed men's interests and status in society. These men's groups focused variously on issues such as defining and restoring men's rights in marriage and divorce; strengthening fathers' rights, including child custody rights; developing stronger laws to defend men against charges of domestic violence; and pursuing judicial support for establishing the right of husbands and sexual partners to prevent a woman from obtaining an abortion without their agreement.

Men's rights proponents make a number of arguments to support their right to participate in abortion decisions. Most focus on what seems to be a profoundly uneven and unfair distribution of power, with women holding too much and men too little. For example, they argue, whereas a man can be forced to accept the legal obligations of paternity, including the financial obligations, he cannot prevent a woman from having an abortion. On the other hand, a woman can decide to end a pregnancy by abortion, and she can also force a man to support a child she gives birth to, even if the pregnancy was unintended or unwanted by the father. Women's rights advocates point out that because pregnancy and delivery carry inherent risks to a woman's health and life, decisions about continuing or ending a pregnancy must always be a woman's decision. The US Supreme Court decision in *Planned Parenthood of Southeast Pennsylvania v. Casey,* denying the requirement that husbands must be notified before the abortion takes place, asserted that "it cannot be claimed that the father's interest in the fetus's welfare is equal to the mother's protected liberty, since it is an inescapable biological fact that state regulation with respect to the fetus will have a far greater impact on the pregnant woman's bodily integrity than it will on the husband."

Women's rights advocates argue that decisions about supporting the child are separate from matters having to do with the conditions of the sexual encounter or even considerations of "sexual responsibility." Once the child is born, then the child's best interests must be paramount, and the mother and father of the child must meet their responsibilities to this person.

How does domestic violence intersect with reproductive issues?

According to the National Coalition against Domestic Violence, one in every four women in the United States will experience domestic violence in her lifetime and more than 1 million women each year are victims of physical assault by an intimate partner. Women between the ages of twenty and twenty-four are at greatest risk. The cost of domestic violence is almost $6 billion a year, mostly for direct medical and psychological services. A number of national and local organizations, many founded in the 1970s by Second Wave feminists, are working to raise public awareness of sexual and domestic violence and to end it.[1]

Male violence against women in all forms—domestic violence, rape and sexual assault, pornography, prostitution, sexual harassment—happens within the context of a society in which men typically exercise greater cultural, economic, and political power than women. Not surprisingly then, today as in the past, many women indicate that their reports of sex- and gender-based violence are dismissed by authorities, an experience that arguably constitutes another layer of sex-based violation. These various forms of violence against women interact with women's reproductive experiences in many different arenas. Statistics show, for instance, a high incidence of male violence against women during pregnancy. Women also face situations in which male sexual partners may sabotage their access to contraception or abortion services. Finally, when men deal with women as sex objects or force them to have sex, especially unprotected sex, one outcome may well be pregnancy or sexually transmitted disease.

21

GLOBAL REPRODUCTIVE HEALTH AND US PROGRAMS AND POLITICS

What is USAID's family-planning program?

The United States Agency for International Development (USAID) is an independent federal agency that provides economic, developmental, and humanitarian assistance around the world in support of the foreign policy goals of the United States. USAID's family-planning programs reside within the agency's Office of Population and Reproductive Health. Since 1965, these programs have supported voluntary family planning, efforts to stabilize population growth, reduction of high-risk pregnancies, child-spacing, reduction of abortion, AIDS education, and distribution of female and male condoms to protect against transmission of infection. The programs have also supported women's rights and opportunities to participate fully in society.

According to USAID, the agency's family-planning programs distribute more than 35 percent of all donor-provided contraceptives to the developing world and have helped bring understanding of contraceptive practices to women and men around the world. USAID has pioneered door-to-door distribution of contraceptives, mobile clinic services, and employment-based health care programs in the developing world. The organization has also trained midwives and other traditional birth attendants to provide family-planning services, among other accomplishments.

Since the enactment of the Helms Amendment in 1973, no USAID funds have been used to support abortion as a method of family planning. USAID works to prevent abortion by teaching about family planning, providing materials, and connecting women with family-planning and health services. The organization also works to save the lives of women who have undergone unsafe abortions.

What are the "global gag rule" and the Helms Amendment?

Soon after *Roe*, Senator Jesse Helms, a Republican from North Carolina, introduced an amendment to the US Foreign Assistance Act, banning all US foreign aid for abortion. The aforementioned Helms Amendment can only be rescinded by an act of Congress; it remains in effect today.

In 1984, during the presidency of Ronald Reagan, the US representative to the International Conference on Population in Mexico City announced that the United States would no longer support nongovernmental organizations (NGOs) that, using their own resources, counsel or advocate abortion or refer individuals to abortion services. The policy also disqualifies foreign NGOs from receiving US family-planning funds if they provide legal abortion services, except in cases of rape, incest, or a pregnancy that is a threat to the woman's life; or if they lobby to make abortion legal or accessible in their country. This executive branch policy, known as the Mexico City Policy—or, by opponents, as the Global Gag Rule—was in effect until Bill Clinton became president in 1993. While the policy was in force, a five-country study showed that cooperating agencies, in fear of violating its rules, were behaving overcautiously, directly limiting access to reproductive health care and family-planning services, thereby leaving women with fewer options overall. Even after the policy was rescinded in 1993, NGOs had to maintain US money for reproductive health services in segregated accounts, to make certain that none of it would be used for abortions.

When George W. Bush became president in 2001, he reinstated the Mexico City Policy on the twenty-eighth anniversary of *Roe v. Wade*. President Bush reaffirmed his allegiance to the policy and attempted various extensions of it until he left office, despite a number of Senate votes against these efforts. The policy also faced the opposition of international health professionals, lawyers, policy makers, NGOs, religious organizations, representatives of the United Nations Population Fund, the World Health Organization, and the World Bank because of its demonstrable, deleterious effects on the health of women around the world.

Following the general pattern of Republican opposition/ Democratic support, Barack Obama rescinded the Mexico City Policy when he became president in 2009. He issued a statement indicating that USAID and State Department grants should exclude gag rule provisions and that current grants should, too, because the policy "undermined efforts to promote safe and effective voluntary family planning in developing countries." President Obama called for cooperation among people on "all sides of the issue," for an end to the politicization of foreign aid for family planning and reproductive health, and for support for programs to reduce unintended pregnancies around the world.

What is the United Nations Population Fund and what relationship does the United States have to this organization?

The recent history of the relationship between the United Nations Population Fund (UNFPA) and the United States government provides another illustration of the enormous impact that reproductive politics within the United States has had on women around the world. UNFPA is the largest internationally funded source of population assistance to developing countries. The organization describes its work as promoting the right of every woman, man, and child to enjoy a life of health and equal opportunity. UNFPA supports policies and programs in about 150 countries that aim to reduce poverty and to ensure that every pregnancy is wanted, every birth is safe, every young person is free of HIV/AIDS, and every woman, young or old, is treated with dignity and respect. For more than forty years, UNFPA has collected voluntary contributions from participating countries and distributed more than $6 billion for use in family-planning, delivery, and other health services.

UNPFA programs target many of the 201 million women around the world who do not have access to effective contraception. Programs also aim to reduce extremely high rates of maternal mortality (536,000 deaths per year, most of which are preventable), to raise rates of prenatal care for the poorest women on earth (about 35 percent of women in poor countries have no contact with health care personnel before delivery), and to slow the spread of HIV/AIDS.

During the Reagan administration, Congress restricted US funding to USFPA because of allegations that the organization sent money to China to fund their involuntary sterilization and forced-abortion programs. (UNPFA has always denied its participation and deplored these practices, and no human rights organization has ever accused UNPFA of these violations in China or other countries.) During subsequent decades, US funding for UNPFA has generally been restored when Democratic presidents are in power and constrained or terminated when Republican presidents are elected and when Republicans control Congress. In 2002, President Bush sent a fact-finding team to China to investigate the connection between UNPFA funds and coercive reproductive practices in that country. The team found no evidence of UNFPA wrongdoing and recommended that the US government fund the organization. Nevertheless, during the administration of George W. Bush, no US funds were contributed to the organization. In 2009 after Barack Obama became president, with the support of a Democrat-controlled Congress, the funding program was restarted, although as political changes occur, US support for international family planning and reproductive health remains insecure, uncertain, and highly politicized.

Is there an international body monitoring women's reproductive health?

The Committee on the Elimination of Discrimination against Women (CEDAW) is the body of independent experts that monitors implementation of the United Nations Convention on the Elimination of All Forms of Discrimination against Women. Countries that are parties to the CEDAW have a duty to ensure maternal health by providing women with appropriate pregnancy services and education about maternity as a "social function." Countries that have high rates of maternal mortality and morbidity may be in violation of this responsibility to women's life, health, equality, and nondiscrimination. The CEDAW Committee considers state refusal to provide legitimate reproductive health services—including by criminalization—a form of discrimination against women and recommends that abortion should be available to victims of rape and incest. Further, the CEDAW maintains that a lack of access to contraceptives impedes women's right to "decide freely and responsibly on the number and spacing of their children"; thus, women across their life span must have information and services regarding contraception as well as sex education.[1]

22

HEALTH CARE AND REPRODUCTIVE POLITICS

What does the federal health care reform act of 2010 say about pregnancy, contraception, abortion, and reproductive health care generally?

The United States has the most expensive health care system of any country in the world. Medical costs per person and the percentage of the gross national product spent on health care are higher than in other wealthy country including Australia, Canada, Germany, the Netherlands, New Zealand, and the United Kingdom. Yet by many measures—access to health care; degree of disparities in care for better-off and less-well-off people; existence of national policies that promote primary, preventive care; and use of information technology—the US health care system has lagged behind the systems in other Western countries.

The US health care system has had particular gaps in the areas of reproductive health services for girls and women. One measure of this is that our teen pregnancy rate is higher than rates in other wealthy, industrialized countries, with long-term negative consequences for many young women when it comes to education and employment opportunities. In addition, in the era before health care reform, approximately 14 million women of childbearing age have lacked health care insurance, or about 22 percent of women in that age group.[1]

Most provisions of the 2010 federal act do not come into effect until 2014, and there is still a complicated set of fundamental challenges for the act to survive before that date. The Supreme Court's June 2012 affirmation of the constitutionality of the Affordable Care Act generally, including the penalty for those who do not meet its requirement that everyone must purchase health care insurance, was an important first step. Still, Republicans holding national office are determined to overturn the act, and many Republican governors have announced that they will not implement the Medicaid expansion designed to increase the number of low-income persons covered. In the meantime, the act's provisions are a good guide to the reproductive health services that Congress has defined as crucial for all women. The health reform act and the debates that preceded and followed its passage are also a good guide to where the political lines are drawn across women's bodies, marking which services are approved and which are not, at this time.

As noted, the federal health reform act has expanded the Medicaid program, allowing more very low income families to have health insurance, but this provision has an uncertain future. The new health exchanges will also allow slightly better-off Americans to purchase subsidized insurance. These expansions could together extend basic coverage to millions of women of childbearing age. In addition, several provisions will address women's sexual and reproductive health before 2014. Adult children under the age of twenty-six, among whom rates of unintended pregnancy and sexually transmitted infections are especially high, can now be covered by their parents' health plans. Upon the bill's passage as well, a larger number of lower income women and men than previously became eligible for Medicaid coverage specifically for family planning.

Other provisions of the act require insurance plans to offer a set of essential health benefits, including maternity care.

This feature will vastly expand the number of women covered during pregnancy. Commencing August 2012, a number of reproduction-related preventative services were covered without copayment, coinsurance, or deductible when a woman uses a plan network provider. This coverage includes preconception and prenatal care; screening for gestational diabetes; counseling and screening for STDs; prenatal and postpartum lactation education and support; subsidy for rental of breast pumps; screening and counseling for interpersonal and domestic violence; and all FDA-approved contraceptive methods, sterilization, and counseling.

Moreover, another group of benefits that are especially important to women has been included in the act. Women will no longer need to obtain a physician's referral to make an appointment for gynecological or obstetric care. Additionally, as I noted earlier, the provision that forbids exclusions based on a "prior condition" means that a woman who has undergone a caesarean delivery cannot subsequently be denied maternity coverage for that reason. Likewise, insurance companies can no longer practice "gender rating," or charging women higher premiums than they charge men.

Economists and other experts have affirmed that these aspects of the health reform act will make pregnancy, family planning, and other female-related health services more accessible and affordable for millions of girls and women, and will contribute to the project of reducing health care costs in general. Yet political opposition to the act remains fierce, and its future is unclear.

The issue of abortion was treated as a toxic element throughout the health care reform debates. In the last stages, the entire bill's passage seemed to depend on a vote to express allegiance to an amendment guaranteeing anti-abortion provisions that had already been in force, via the Hyde Amendment, since 1978. In the end, the act lays out rules that segregate insurance premiums so that no federal funds can fund abortion. States are still free to enact their own funding prohibitions. In 2010,

Arizona, Louisiana, Mississippi, Missouri, and Tennessee passed laws prohibiting abortion coverage in plans purchased through the exchanges. A number of other states have passed variants of these laws.

Why did abortion become so controversial during congressional health care debates?

In 2009, Representative Bart Stupak (D-MI) introduced an anti-abortion amendment to the House health care reform bill, barring public and private health insurers from covering abortion if the plans accepted subscribers who received public subsidies to help pay for their insurance. The amendment was approved by a bi-partisan majority.

The Stupak amendment was consistent with a number of pre- and post-*Roe v. Wade* political strategies that have used women's reproductive capacities to achieve political goals that have little or nothing to do with women's interests. Severe restrictions on abortion funding would not, for example, lead to a more effective or streamlined health care system for anyone in the United States. Nor would these provisions serve women in particular whose health and capacity to earn a living may be compromised by pregnancy, childbirth, and child rearing. While some representatives who oppose abortion on religious grounds may have had no larger agenda than securing religious dicta, others turned women's reproductive needs into a weapon against health care reform. In addition, the Hyde Amendment had long forbidden the use of federal funds for abortion.

In 2009, Representative Stupak and his supporters were not so constrained. Stupak's amendment curtailed the reproductive rights of poor women *and* middle-class women who depend on their health insurance. In this way, the supporters of the Stupak Amendment transformed abortion into a national issue in an entirely new way. No longer only a "women's issue," or even, after the Stupak Amendment, simply for some a religious issue, abortion became the linch-pin that the rise or fall of health care reform depended on. Everyone's life in America, via health care legislation, was now connected to abortion.

Even after the passage of the Health Care and Education Reconciliation Act of 2010, anti-abortion members of Congress, stimulated by the success of the Stupak Amendment, contin-ued to attempt to eliminate access to and coverage for abor-tion. Congress passed H.R. 3 in 2011, which aimed to create mandates and tax penalties for families, military personnel, and small businesses that use private funds to buy insurance plans that include abortion coverage. H.R. 3 would also have limited coverage of abortions for rape victims to only those who could prove *forcible* rape, among other provisions.

23

LANGUAGE AND FRAMEWORKS

When did Americans adopt the language of
"choice" and "right to life"?

During the late 1960s and early 1970s, advocates of legal abortion used the term "rights," much more frequently than "choice," to refer to what they were trying to achieve. However, *choice* still had a place in this early discourse. For example, the National Abortion Rights Action League's first national action in 1969—a Mother's Day demonstration held in conjunction with press conferences in eleven cities—was called "Children by Choice." Others referred prominently to *Roe v. Wade* as "a great day for freedom of choice." But in the years before *Roe,* most activists explained that the *right* to decide whether or not to stay pregnant was indivisible from the *right* to self-determination.

The transition to *choice* came from several sources. First, Justice Blackmun referred to abortion as "this choice" a number of times in his *Roe v. Wade* majority ruling, terminology that acknowledged, in part, the impact of the women's movement. The language of *choice* centered reproductive experiences in the domain of women's bodies, and validated women's needs to respond to their reproductive capacities within the context of their whole lives. Also, abortion rights activists were determined to develop a respectable, nonconfrontational movement after *Roe v. Wade.* Many proponents wanted to adopt the term *choice* because they realized that some people in the United States were weary of—or hostile to—*rights* claims after the civil rights movement. Many people believed that *choice*, a term that evoked women as individuals, not as an activist mass—even as women shoppers selecting among options in the marketplace—would offer a kind of "rights lite," a less threatening package than unadulterated *reproductive rights*.

Anti-abortion groups selected the affirming, fetus-focused term *right to life* to oppose the individualist, consumerist, and women-centered term "choice." "Right to life" directly addressed the rights-claiming culture of the era and is usually understood as ascribing human status and human rights to the zygote from the moment of conception. The language drew in part on the Declaration of Independence, which weaves together religion, patriotism, justice, and an eighteenth-century white masculine vision of human rights when it states, "We hold these truths to be self-evident, that all men are created equal, that they are endowed by their Creator with certain unalienable Rights, that among these are Life, Liberty and the pursuit of Happiness." Two decades after *Roe v. Wade*, Pope John Paul II invoked "the culture of life" to denounce abortion and euthanasia, exemplars of "the culture of death."

Critics of "right to life" language have pointed out that many people with anti-abortion views are in favor of the death penalty, oppose universal access to health care, and oppose public assistance for poor mothers and children, all of which can lead to deaths preventable by laws and public policies that value life above all.

Historically the term "rights" has been used to refer to privileges or benefits to which a person is justly entitled and that can be exercised without access to any special resources, such as money. In the United States, some groups have had to mount long campaigns to demand access to rights that other groups, usually white men, could exercise because of their demographic characteristics. For example, women and African Americans in the United States struggled for and won *voting rights*, that is, the right of all citizens over a certain age to vote, even if they have no money, no property, and no other resources.

By contrast, *choice* has come to be intimately connected to the possession of resources. Many Americans believe that women who exercise choice are supposed to be legitimate consumers possessing money, even when the choices they exercise, such as the choice to become a mother or the choice to end a pregnancy, might be considered a very fundamental issue of rights. In the 1980s and 1990s, anti-welfare politicians, for example, concentrated on portraying poor women who had children as bad choice makers, as women who had no business having babies.

Choice has come to connote the privilege to exercise discrimination in the marketplace among several options, if one has the wherewithal to enter the marketplace to begin with. As a consequence, and during a period when babies—and pregnancy itself—have become ever-more commodified, women with financial resources have been defined as having a legitimate relationship to babies and motherhood status, while poorer women have been defined as illegitimate consumers with no right to choose motherhood. These distinctions emerged quickly in the post-rights era of *choice*, and eclipsed the connection of women's reproductive autonomy to *rights*, which undermined the possibility that all women would be equally empowered by *reproductive choice*. Dividing women into good and bad choice makers gave cultural and political strength to the idea that reproductive options, including motherhood, should be a class privilege reserved for the good choice makers because they can afford the choices they make.

Do various groups of women interpret their needs regarding fertility and reproduction uniquely and if so, why does this matter?

Since the 1960s, mainstream reproductive choice organizations have spent the majority of their time and resources trying to build legislative, judicial, and popular support for the right of girls and women to use contraceptives, obtain abortions, and achieve widespread access to these tools of reproductive choice. In the early years of these efforts, a number of women of color organizations realized they had to focus their work more broadly. For example, many middle-class white activists, resisting their physicians' control, argued in the 1960s and 1970s that the right to choose sterilization was an important component of reproductive autonomy and that women ought to be free to undergo the procedure without waiting periods or other physician-imposed tests. Simultaneously, the National Black Feminist Organization, the Committee to End Sterilization Abuse, and other organizations built their efforts around advocating *for* waiting periods, along with informed consent rules, and other protections for women of color who had historically been targets of coercive reproductive practices including forced sterilization programs.

In the generation after *Roe v. Wade*, middle-class women and the organizations they supported claimed women's rights to use any contraceptive they chose, and pursued legal actions against drug companies to hold them to account for the safety of their contraceptive products. At the same time, women of color organizations focused on building opposition to the Hyde Amendment that forbade the use of Medicaid funds for abortion. They also constructed campaigns to oppose health- and court-ordered mandates deploying Depo-Provera and other long-acting, reversible contraceptives to constrain the "undesirable" reproductive activity of young women of color and women eligible for public assistance who, according to politicians and others, were producing too many children. In addition, in the 1980s, 1990s, and into this century, organizations and individuals representing the interests of poor women and women of color conducted campaigns to claim the reproductive health and dignity of these groups by developing access to comprehensive reproductive health care and protection from hazardous, low-wage employment and from exposure to environmental toxins, as well as protection from human trafficking.

Historically, mainstream organizations largely founded and run by white, middle-class women concentrated on basic and essential, if narrowly defined, needs of all women. For some decades, these high-profile organizations tended to neglect or make secondary their efforts to support the broader requirements of women whose reproductive health, safety, and even their right to be mothers were threatened and constrained by a society that didn't value all women and children equally. Consequently, the task of building an inclusive movement and legal structures that recognize and work for the rights of all women to manage their own reproductive capacity and to be mothers or not has been a difficult undertaking. Even today, the political culture in the United States supports the reproductive rights of women who have abundant resources far more than it supports the rights of women with few resources.

However, mainstream organizations have become more attentive than in the past to building campaigns that attend to the reproductive needs of all women. In addition, there are many political organizations that work specifically to secure the reproductive health, safety, and dignity of women whose access to such protections has historically been marginalized. These include the National Women's Health Network, the National Network of Abortion Funds, Black Women for Reproductive Justice, Asian Communities for Reproductive Justice, the National Latina Institute for Reproductive Health, the National Asian Pacific American Women's Forum, the Civil Liberties and Public Policy Program at Hampshire College, and the National Advocates for Pregnant Women.

What is "reproductive justice"?

Led by women of color organizations, particularly Sister-Song, an umbrella organization founded in the 1990s by

Loretta Ross, the reproductive justice movement regards women's right to reproduce as a foundational human right. Reproductive justice claims that a woman has the right to be recognized as a legitimate reproducer regardless of race, religion, sexual orientation, economic status, age, immigration status, citizenship status, disability status, and status as an incarcerated woman. The agenda of the reproductive justice movement makes three broad claims:

First, that women have the right to manage their reproductive capacity, including

1. The right to decide whether to become a mother and when;
2. The right to primary culturally competent preventative health care;
3. The right to accurate information about sexuality and reproduction;
4. The right to accurate contraceptive information;
5. The right and access to safe, respectful, and affordable contraceptive materials and services;
6. The right to abortion and access to full information about safe, respectful, affordable abortion services;
7. The right to and equal access to the benefits of and information about the potential risks of reproductive technology.

Second, that women have the right to adequate information, resources, services and personal safety while pregnant, including

1. The right and access to safe, respectful, and affordable medical care during and after pregnancy including treatment for HIV/AIDS, drug and alcohol addiction, and other chronic conditions; and the right

to seek medical care during pregnancy without fear of criminal prosecution or medical interventions against the pregnant woman's will;

2. The right of incarcerated women to safe and respectful care during and after pregnancy, including the right to give birth in a safe, respectful, medically appropriate environment;

3. The right and access to economic security, including the right to earn a living wage;

4. The right to physical safety, including the right to adequate housing and structural protections against rape and sexual violence;

5. The right to practice religion or not, freely and safely, so that authorities cannot coerce women to undergo medical interventions that conflict with their religious convictions;

6. The right to be pregnant in an environmentally safe context;

7. The right to decide among birthing options and access to those services.

Finally, a woman has the right to be the parent of her child, which includes

1. The right to economic resources sufficient to be a parent, including the right to earn a living wage;

2. The right to education and training in preparation for earning a living wage;

3. The right to decide whether or not to be the parent of the child one gives birth to;

4. The right to parent in a physically and environmentally safe context;

5. The right to leave work to care for newborns or others in need of care;

6. The right to affordable, high-quality child care.

What contemporary, contested frameworks are structuring reproductive politics today?

The growing coalition in support of reproductive justice faces a political culture that is bitterly split regarding reproductive politics. Like Medicaid in 1965 and *Roe v. Wade* in 1973, the national health care project has become an arena for sharpening debates about the federal government's role in facilitating women's ability to control their fertility. We've seen that an anti-abortion amendment nearly derailed congressional approval for the Affordable Care Act of 2010. Later as struggles over the political feasibility of a national health care system continued, contraception replaced abortion at the crux of conflict.

In January 2012 President Obama announced that most health insurance plans must cover contraception for women free of charge, a rule that twenty-eight states had already adopted. The president's directive reflected the intent of the 2010 act which says that insurers must cover "preventative health services," in this case all FDA-approved contraceptives, emergency contraception, and sterilization, and cannot charge for them—no copays, no deductibles.

After fierce objections from Catholic-affiliated institutions such as universities, hospitals, and social service agencies, the Obama administration promised that students and employees, many not Catholic, who received health insurance through Catholic institutions, would have access to contraceptives while accommodating the religious liberty interests of those institutions. In practical terms, the government proposed that the Catholic institutions would not have to pay for or provide contraception; rather, it would be provided directly from the insurance or pharmaceutical company, for free. The proposed compromise applied to insurance plans that are underwritten by private insurers such as Blue Cross/Blue Shield and did not seem to account for the fact that many of the Catholic institutions in question serve as their own insurers, providing health care coverage directly to employees and paying claims themselves, often a more economical option for large organizations.

The US Conference of Catholic Bishops, vowing to protect the "conscience rights" of institutions and individuals and to defend the very essence of religious liberty in this country, objected to President Obama's directive as forcing the Church to act against its teachings. Also, the bishops objected to the situation they called "an unwarranted government definition of religion," with government deciding which institutions are religious employers deserving exemption from the law.[1] In May 2012, forty-three Roman Catholic dioceses, schools, and social service agencies and other institutions filed lawsuits in twelve federal courts challenging the directive that students and employees at Catholic institutions must have insured access to contraception. By this point, many conservative evangelical groups had joined with the Roman Catholic bishops and others, claiming that by its directive regarding contraception, the government had declared war on religion.

Participants in this debate rarely noted that all Americans, religious or not, have contributed to taxpayer-funded contraceptive services for many years; in 2010 public expenditures for family planning services totaled $2.37 billion. More than 17 million women—nearly half of all women who needed these services—qualified for publicly funded services and supplies because they had incomes below 250 percent of the federal poverty level or they were younger than twenty.[2]

As of summer 2012, a majority of Catholics did not believe that the right to religious liberty was threatened by the directive on contraception. In addition, a majority of Catholics believed that employers should be required to provide their employees with health plans that cover contraception at no cost. White Catholics are, however, more divided on these questions than others.[3] Meanwhile, as we've seen, among all women who have had heterosexual sex, 99 percent have ever used a contraceptive method other than natural family planning. This figure is virtually the same among Catholic women (98 percent).[4]

Arguably, American attitudes and behavior regarding contraception suggest that the majority believe in the right of government to set up rules for the common good. Further, a majority of Americans seem to agree that, as a professor of philosophy at Notre Dame University put it, "not every effort of the government to restrict religious rights should be rejected on the grounds that it is a step toward the total undermining of religion."[5] Finally, women's behavior reflects a broad consensus that contraception is a necessary component of women's health care needs. Nevertheless, the debate is fierce and still raging: is the contraception directive a massive assault on religious liberty or a basic building block of a comprehensive health care package for women? This question and others that I've highlighted throughout this book remain unresolved and may stay that way into the foreseeable future.

NOTES

Preface

1. "In Brief: Facts on Unintended Pregnancy in the United States" (New York: Guttmacher Institute, January 2012).

Chapter 2

1 John Bartlow Martin, "Abortion." Parts 1–3, *Saturday Evening Post* (May 20, 1961): 19ff; (May 27, 1961): 20ff; (June 2, 1961): 25ff; Christopher Tietze, "Two Years' Experience with Liberal Abortion Law: Its Impact on Fertility Trends in New York City," *Family Planning Perspectives* 5(1973): 36–41; "In Brief: Facts on Induced Abortion in the United States" (New York: Guttmacher Institute, January 2011).

2. Janet Farrell Brodie, *Contraception and Abortion in 19th Century America* (Ithaca: Cornell University Press, 1994), Chapter 7.

3. Sucheta Mazumdar, "What Happened to the Women? Chinese and Indian Male Migration to the United States in Global Perspective," in Shirley Hune and Gail M. Nomura, eds., *Asian/Pacific Islander American Women: A Historical Anthology* (New York: New York University Press, 2003), 60.

4. Rebecca M. Kluchin, *Fit to Be Tied; Sterilization and Reproductive Rights in America, 1950–1980* (New Brunswick, NJ: Rutgers University Press, 2009), 2.

5. David J. Garrow, *Liberty and Sexuality: The Right to Privacy and the Making of* Roe v. Wade (New York: Macmillan, 1994), 42–43.

6. Rosalind Pollack Petchesky, *Abortion and Woman's Choice: The State, Sexuality, and Reproductive Freedom,* rev. ed. (Boston: Northeastern University Press, 1990), 159–160.

7. Elena Gutiérrez, *Fertile Matters: The Politics of Mexican-Origin Women's Reproduction* (Austin: University of Texas Press, 2008).

8. Garrow, 513.

9. Laura Kaplan, *The Story of Jane: The Legendary Underground Feminist Abortion Service* (Chicago: University of Chicago Press, 1997).

10. Linda Gordon, *The Moral Property of Women: A History of Birth Control Politics in America* (Urbana: University of Illinois Press, 2002), 25.

11. Rachel Benson Gold, "Abortion and Women's Health" (New York: Guttmacher Institute, 1990).

12. Linda Greenhouse and Reva Siegel, "Before (and After) *Roe v. Wade*: New Questions about Backlash," *Yale Law Journal* 28(2011): 2028–2087.

13. Carole Joffe, *Dispatches from the Abortion Wars: The Cost of Fanaticism to Doctors, Patients and the Rest of Us* (Boston: Beacon Press, 2010), 47–49.

14. Ibid., Chapter 3.

Chapter 3

1. Andrea Tone, *Devices and Desires: A History of Contraceptives in America* (New York: Hill and Wang, 2001), 135.

Chapter 4

1. Richard Lincoln, Brigette Doring-Bradley, Barbara L. Lindheimand, and Maureen A. Cotterill, "The Court, the Congress, and the

President: Turning Back the Clock on the Pregnant Poor," *Family Planning Perspectives* 9(September–October, 1977): 211.

Chapter 5

1. John R. Connery, *Abortion, the Development of the Roman Catholic Perspective* (Chicago: Loyola University Press, 1977).

2. James Mohr, *Abortion in America: The Origins and Evolution of National Policy* (New York: Oxford University Press, 1978), 186.

3. John L. Allen, Jr., "The Pope v. the Pill," *New York Times*, July 27, 2008.

4. "The Facts Tell the Story: Catholics for Choice" (Washington, DC: Catholics for Choice, 2011).

5. "Characteristics of U.S. Abortion Patients, 2008" (New York: Guttmacher Institute, 2010).

6. K. M. Hedayat, P. Shooshtarizadeh, and M. Raza, "Therapeutic Abortion in Islam: Contemporary Views of Muslim Shiite Scholars and Effects of Recent Iranian Legislation," *Journal of Medical Ethics*, 32(November 2006): 652–657; Heather Boonstra, "Islam, Women and Family Planning: A Primer" Guttmacher Report on Public Policy 4(December 2001) 1–6.

7. Amy Adamczyk, "Understanding the Effects of Personal and School Religiosity on the Decision Not to Abort a Premarital Pregnancy," *Journal of Health and Social Behavior* 50(June 2009): 180–195.

Chapter 6

1. "U.S. Population Projections, 2005–2050" (Washington, DC: Pew Research Center, February 11, 2008).

2. "Public Favors Border Controls and Path to Citizenship; Most Oppose Ending Birthright Citizenship" (Washington, DC: Pew Research Center, February 24, 2011).

3. Jeffrey Passel, Gretchen Livingston, and D'Vera Cohn, "Explaining Why Minority Births Now Outnumber White Births," Pew Social and Demographic Trends (Washington, DC: Pew Research Center, May 17, 2012).

4. Damian Cave, "Better Lives for Mexican Citizens Cut Allure of Going North," *New York Times*, July 6, 2011; Lesley Sapp, "Apprehensions by the U.S. Border Patrol: 2005–2010," Factsheet, Policy Directorate, Office of Immigration Statistics (Washington, DC: US Department of Homeland Security, July 2011).

5. "The Human Right to Health and Women's Reproductive Health Policy," *Ipas*, February 2009.

Chapter 7

1. Marisa Chappell, *The War on Welfare: Family, Poverty and Policy in Modern America* (Philadelphia: University of Pennsylvania Press, 2009), 168; Heather Bushey, "The New Breadwinners," in *Shriver Report* (Washington, DC: Center for American Progress, 2009).

2. Rebecca Ray, Janet C. Gornick, and John Schmitt, "Parental Leave Policies in 21 Countries: Assessing Generosity and Gender Equality" (Washington, DC: Center for Economic and Policy Research, rev. June 2009).

3. "Women's Lower Wages Worsen Their Circumstances in a Difficult Economy" (Washington, DC: National Women's Law Center, April 2010).

4. Jeanne Flavin and Lynn M. Paltrow, "Punishing Pregnant Drug-Using Women: Defying Law, Medicine, and Common Sense," *Journal of Addictive Diseases* 29(2010): 231–244.

5. Susan Okie, "The Epidemic That Wasn't," *New York Times*, January 6, 2009, citing the National Institutes of Health's "The Maternal Lifestyle Study."

6. Gwendolyn Mink and Rickie Solinger, eds., *WELFARE* (New York: New York University Press, 2002).

7. "Disproportionality: Addressing Racial Disproportionality in Child Welfare," Child Welfare Information Gateway, Administration for Children and Families (Washington, DC: US Department of Health and Human Services, January 2011); "The AFCARS Report," Administration on Children, Youth and Families, Children's Bureau (Washington, DC: US Department of Health and Human Services, July 2009).

8. Dorothy Roberts, *Shattered Bonds: The Color of Child Welfare* (New York: Basic Books, 2002).

Chapter 8

1. Brady E. Hamilton and Stephanie J. Ventura, "Birth Rates for U.S. Teenagers Reach Historic Lows for All Ages and Ethnic Groups," NCHS Data Brief, 89 (Atlanta, GA: Centers for Disease Control and Prevention, April 2012).

2. Stephanie J. Ventura, "Changing Patterns of Nonmarital Childbearing in the United States," Division of Vital Statistics, NCHS Data Brief, No. 18 (Atlanta, GA: Centers for Disease Control and Prevention, May 2009).

3. Robert Rector, "Marriage: America's Greatest Weapon against Child Poverty," Backgrounder #2465 (Washington, DC: Heritage Foundation, September 16, 2010).

4. Kathryn Edin and Maria Kefalas, *Promises I Can Keep: Why Poor Women Put Motherhood before Marriage* (Berkeley: University of California Press, 2005).

5. Marybeth J. Mattingly and Jessica A. Bean, "The Unequal Distribution of Child Poverty: Highest Rates among Young Blacks and Children of Single Mothers in Rural America," Issue Brief, No. 18 (Durham, NH: Carsey Institute, Fall 2010).

6. Caroline Ratcliffe and Signe-Mary McKernan, "Childhood Poverty Persistence: Facts and Consequences" (Washington, DC: Urban Institute, 2010).

Chapter 9

1. M. Hogben, H. Chesson, and S. O. Aral, "Sexuality Education Policies and Sexually Transmitted Disease Rates in the United States of America," *International Journal of STD and AIDS* 4(2010): 293–297.

2. Sara Dubow, *Ourselves Unborn: A History of the Fetus in Modern America* (New York: Oxford University Press, 2011).

3. Brian Powell, Catherine Bolzendahl, Claudia Geist, Lala Carr Steelman, *Counted Out: Same-Sex Relations and America's Definition of Family*. American Sociological Association's Rose Series in Sociology (Washington, DC: American Sociological Association, 2010).

Chapter 10

1. "Facts on Contraceptive Use in the United States" (New York: Guttmacher Institute, June 2010).

2. "Facts on Publicly Funded Contraceptive Services in the United States" (New York: Guttmacher Institute, May 2012).

3. Emily Monea, and Adam Thomas, "Unintended Pregnancy and Taxpayer Spending," *Perspectives on Sexual and Reproductive Health* 43(2011): 88–93.

Chapter 11

1. "In Brief: Facts on Induced Abortion in the United States" (New York: Guttmacher Institute, January 2011).

2. Pew Research Center, "Do you think abortion should be legal in all cases, legal in most cases, illegal in most cases, or illegal in all cases?" April 4–15, 2012.

3. Vignetta E. Charles., Chelsea Polis, Srinvas Sridhara, and R. W. Blum, "Abortion and Long-term Mental Health Outcomes:

A Systematic Review of the Evidence," *Contraception* 78(2008): 436–450.

4. Brenda Major, Mark Appelbaum, Linda Beckman, Mary Ann Dutton, Nancy Felipe Russo, and Carolyn West, *American Psychologist* 64(December 2009): 863–890.

5. "Abortion, Miscarriage, and Breast Cancer Risk," National Cancer Institute FactSheet (Washington, DC: US National Institutes of Health, 2010).

Chapter 12

1. Rachel K. Jones and Kathryn Kooistra, "Abortion Incidence and Access to Services in the United States, 2008," *Perspectives on Sexual and Reproductive Health* 43(2011): 41–50; "Long-Term Decline in Abortions Has Stalled" (New York: Guttmacher Institute, March 11, 2011).

2. "Facts on Induced Abortion in the United States" (New York: Guttmacher Institute, January 2011).

3. Ibid.

4. Susan A. Cohen, "Abortion and Women of Color: The Bigger Picture," *Guttmacher Policy Review* 11(Summer 2008): 1–4; "Abortion Has Become More Concentrated among Poor Women," Media Center (New York: Guttmacher Institute, May 4, 2010).

5. "Abortion Has Become More Concentrated among Poor Women"; Lori Freedman, Uta Landy, Philip Darney, and Jody Steinauer "Obstacles to the Integration of Abortion into Obstetrics and Gynecology Practice," *Perspectives on Sexual and Reproductive Health* 42(2010): 146–151.

6. Carole Joffe, *Dispatches from the Abortion Wars.*

7. "Are You in the Know? Abortion and Abortion Providers" (New York: Guttmacher Institute, January 2012).

8. Eve Espey, Tony Ogburn, Alice Chavez, Clifford Qualls, and Mario Leyba, "Abortion Education in Medical Schools: A National Survey," *American Journal of Obstetrics and Gynecology* 192(2005): 640–643.

Chapter 13

1. "State Policies in Brief: Counseling and Waiting Periods for Abortion" (New York: Guttmacher Institute, May 1, 2012).

Chapter 14

1. Harper Jean Tobin, "Confronting Misinformation on Abortion: Informed Consent, Deference, and Fetal Pain Laws," *Columbia Journal of Gender and Law* 17(2008): 111–152.

Chapter 15

1. National Vital Statistics Reports, 60(November 3, 2011), Table 15, Centers for Disease Control and Prevention (Hyattsville, MD: US Department of Health and Human Services); R. Bradley Sears, Gary Gates, and William B. Rubenstein, "Same-Sex Couples and Same-Sex Couples Raising Children in the United States," Williams Project on Sexual Orientation, Law, and Public Policy (Los Angeles: UCLA School of Law, September 2005).

2. A. Chandra, G. M. Martinez, W. D. Mosher, J. C. Abma, and J. Jones, "Fertility, Family Planning, and Reproductive Health of the United States, Women: Data from the 2002 National Survey of Family Growth," Tables 67, 69, 97, *Vital Health Statistics* 23 (December 2005): 1–160.

Chapter 16

1. "Policy Perspective: Keeping the Promises" (New York: Evan B. Donaldson Institute, October 2010).

2. Ibid.; Susan Smith, "Safeguarding the Rights and Well-Being of Birthparents" (New York: Evan B. Donaldson Institute, January 2007).

3. Dorothy Roberts, *Shattered Bonds: The Color of Child Welfare* (New York: Basic Books, 2002); "Disproportionality: Addressing the Disproportionate Number of Children and Youth of Color in Foster Care and the Inequitable Outcomes They Experience" (Washington, DC: National Foster Care Coalition, 2007).

4. Diane Marr and Laura Briggs, eds., *International Adoption: Global Inequalities and the Circulation of Children* (New York: New York University Press, 2009), Introduction, 1–21; "Table 12, Immigrant Orphans Adopted by U.S. Citizens by Gender, Age, and Region and Country of Birth: Fiscal Year 2009," Yearbook of Immigration Statistics, Office of Immigration Statistics (Washington, DC: US Department of Homeland Security, 2009).

5. Jo Jones, "Who Adopts? Characteristics of Women and Men Who Have Adopted Children," NCHS Data Brief, 12 (Atlanta, GA: Centers for Disease Control and Prevention, January 2009).

6. Dorothy Roberts, *Killing the Black Body: Race, Reproduction, and the Meaning of Liberty* (New York: Pantheon, 1997).

Chapter 17

1. "Girl Disrupted: Hormone Disruptors and Women's Reproductive Health, a Report on Women's Reproductive Health and the Environment Workshop," (Bolinas, CA: Collaborative on Health and the Environment, Commonweal, January 2009); see Kristen Iversen, *Full Body Burden: Growing Up in the Shadow of Rocky Flats* (New York: Crown, 2012).

2. T. J. Woodruff, A. R. Zola, and J. M. Schwartz, "Environmental Chemicals in Pregnant Women in the U.S.: NHANES 2003–2004," *Environmental Health Perspectives* 119(June 2011): 878–885.

3. See, for example, Robert Bullard, ed., *The Quest for Environmental Justice: Human Rights and the Politics of Pollution* (San Francisco: Sierra Club Books, 2005).

Chapter 18

1. "Reproductive Rights and Women with Disabilities: A Human Rights Framework" (New York: Center for Reproductive Rights, 2002).

2. "The Disability Rights Critique of Prenatal Genetic Testing: Reflections and Recommendations," a Special Supplement to the *Hastings Center Report,* September-October 1999, Garrison, NY.

3. "Generations Ahead/Bridging the Divide: Disability Rights and Reproductive Rights and Justice Advocates Discussing Genetic Technologies" (Oakland, CA: Generations Ahead, 2008).

Chapter 19

1. Michelle J.K. Osterman and Joyce A. Martin, "Epidural and Spinal Anesthesia Use during Labor: 27-State Reporting Area, 2008," *National Vital Statistics Reports* 59(April 6, 2011): 1–13, 16.

2. "Birth Center or Hospital Birth," www.pregnancyandchildren.com.

3. Fay Menacker and Brady E. Hamilton, "Recent Trends in Cesarean Delivery in the United States," NCHS Data Brief, 35 (Atlanta, GA: Centers for Disease Control and Prevention, March 2010).

4. D. B. Ehrenthal, X. Jiang, and D. M. Strobino, "Labor Induction and the Risk of a Cesarean Delivery among Nulliparous Women at Term," *Obstetrics and Gynecology* 116(July 2010): 35–42.

5. "Vaginal Birth after Cesarean: New Insights," Agency for Healthcare Research and Quality, Publication 10-E003 (Washington, DC: US Department of Health and Human Services, March 2010).

6. "Deadly Delivery: The Maternal Healthcare Crisis in the USA" (New York: Amnesty International, 2010).

7. "Does Mother's Milk Transfer Environmental Toxins to Breast-Feeding Babies?" *Scientific American,* January 26, 2010.

Chapter 20

1. "Domestic Violence Facts" (Washington, DC: National Coalition against Domestic Violence, 2007).

Chapter 21

1. CEDAW Committee, General Recommendation 24, Women and Health, UN Doc. A/54/38 1999; The Special Rapporteur on the Right to Health, Report of the Special Rapporteur on the Right of Everyone to the Enjoyment of the Highest Attainable Standard of Physical and Mental Health, delivered to the United Nations General Assembly, October 19, 2006, New York.

Chapter 22

1. "Focus on Health Reform, Impact of Health Reform on Women's Access to Coverage and Care" (Menlo Park, CA: Henry Kaiser Family Foundation, December 2010).

Chapter 23

1. "Bishops Promise to Continue 'Vigorous Efforts' against HHS Violations of Religious Freedom in Health Care Reform Mandate," United States Conference of Catholic Bishops, March 14, 2012.
2. In Brief: Fact Sheet, "Facts on Publicly Funded Contraceptive Services in the United States" (New York: Guttmacher Institute, May 2012).
3. "Fact Sheet: Catholics and New Battle Lines over Religious Liberty" (Washington, DC: Public Religion Research Institute, June 13, 2012).

4. Rachel K. Jones and Joerg Dreweke, "Countering Conventional Wisdom: Religion and Contraceptive Use" (New York: Guttmacher Institute, April 13, 2011).

5. Gary Gutting, "Do the Bishops Have a Case against Obama," Opinionator: The Stone, *New York Times Online*, May 31, 2012.

SUGGESTED READINGS

Though the readings are loosely organized into categories, many of them deal with subjects that cross a number of these categories.

History of Reproductive Politics in the United States

Briggs, Laura. *Reproducing Empire: Race, Sex, Sciece, and U.S. Imperialism in Puerto Rico* (Berkeley: University of California Press, 2002).

Kline, Wendy. *Building a Better Race: Gender, Sexuality, and Eugenics from the Turn of the Century to the Baby Boom* (Berkeley: University of California Press, 2005).

Mohr, James R. *Abortion in America: The Origins and Evolution of National Policy* (New York: Oxford University Press, 1978).

Reagan, Leslie. *When Abortion Was a Crime: Women, Medicine, and Law in the United States* (Berkeley: University of California Press, 1997).

Solinger, Rickie. *Pregnancy and Power: A Short History of Reproductive Politics in America* (New York: New York University Press, 2005).

Tone, Andrea. *Devices and Desires: A History of Contraceptives in America* (New York: Hill and Wang, 2001).

Feminism and Reproductive Politics

Gordon, Linda. *The Moral Property of Women: A History of Birth Control Politics in America* (Urbana: University of Illinois Press, 2002).

Kaplan, Laura. *The Story of Jane: The Legendary Underground Feminist Abortion Service* (New York: Pantheon, 1995).

Nelson, Jennifer. *Women of Color and the Reproductive Rights Movement* (New York: New York University Press, 2003).

Petchesky, Rosalind Pollack. *Abortion and Women's Choice: The State, Sexuality, and Reproductive Freedom* (Boston: Northeastern University Press, 1984).

The Legal Context

Ehrenreich, Nancy. *The Reproductive Rights Reader: Law, Medicine, and the Construction of Motherhood* (New York: New York University Press, 2008).

Garrow, David. *Liberty and Sexuality: The Right to Privacy and the Making of* Roe v. Wade (New York: Macmillan, 1994).

Greenhouse, Linda, and Reva B. Siegel. *Before* Roe v. Wade *Voices that Shaped the Abortion Debate before the Supreme Court's Ruling* (New York: Kaplan, 2010).

Guitton, Stephanie, and Peter Irons, eds. *May It Please the Court: Arguments on Abortions, Transcripts of Eight Supreme Court Oral Arguments on Reproductive Rights* (New York: New Press, 1995).

Norse, Victoria F. *In Reckless Hands:* Skinner v. Oklahoma *and the Near-Triumph of American Eugenics* (New York: W.W. Norton, 2008).

Roberts, Dorothy. *Killing the Black Body: Race, Reproduction, and the Meaning of Liberty* (New York: Pantheon, 1997).

Siegal, Reva B. "Abortion as a Sex Equality Right: Its Basis in Feminist Theory," in Martha Albertson Fineman and Isabel Karpin (eds.), *Mothers in Law: Feminist Theory and the Legal Regulation of Motherhood* (New York: Routledge, 1995).

Abortion

Joffe, Carole. *Dispatches from the Abortion Wars: The Costs of Fanaticism to Doctors, Patients, and the Rest of Us* (Boston: Beacon Press, 2009).

Mason, Carol. *Killing for Life: The Apocalyptic Narrative of Pro-Life Politics* (Ithaca, NY: Cornell University Press, 2002).

Rose, Melody. *Safe, Legal, and Unavailable? Abortion Politics in the United States* (Washington, DC: CQ Press, 2006).

Tribe, Lawrence. Abortion: The Clash of Absolutes (New York: W.W. Norton, 1992).

Guttmacher Institute, periodicals, fact sheets, reports.

Religion and Reproductive Politics

Jones, Rachel K., and Joerg Dreweke. "Countering Conventional Wisdom: New Evidence on Religion and Contraceptive Use" (New York: Guttmacher Institute, 2011).

Religious Coalition for Reproductive Choice. "In Good Conscience: Guidelines for the Ethical Provision of Health Care in a Pluralistic Society" (Washington, DC: Religious Coalition for Reproductive Choice, April 25, 2007).

Family

Bernstein, Mary, and Reimann, Renate, eds. *Queer Families, Queer Politics: Challenging Culture and the State* (New York: Columbia University Press, 2001).

Coontz, Stephanie, ed., with Maya Parson and Gabrielle Raley. *American Families: A Multicultural Reader* (New York: Routledge, 2nd ed., 2008).

Population Issues

Center for Reproductive Rights. "Rethinking Population Policies: A Reproductive Rights Framework" (New York: Center for Reproductive Rights, 2003).

Goldberg, Michelle. *The Means of Reproduction: Sex, Power, and The Future of the World* (New York: Penguin Press, 2009).

Priscilla Huang. "Anchor Babies, Over-Breeders, and the Population Bomb: The Reemergence of Nativism and Population Control in Anti-Immigration Policies," *Harvard Law and Policy Review* 2 (2008): 385–406.

Drug Use, Punishment, and Reproductive Politics

"Caught in the Net: The Impact of Drug Policies on Women and Families," ACLU, Break the Chains: Communities of Color and the War on Drugs, and The Brennan Center at NYU School of Law, 2005.

Paltrow, Lynn. "Punishment and Prejudice: Judging Drug-Using Pregnant Women," in Julia E. Hanigsber and Sara Ruddick, eds., *Mother Troubles, Rethinking Contemporary Maternal Dilemmas* (Boston: Beacon Press, 1999).

Lynn M. Paltrow and Kathrine D. Jack, "Pregnant Women, Junk Science, and Zealous Defense," *The Champion* 30 (May 2010), 1–18.

Poverty and Reproduction

Center for Reproductive Rights. "Whose Choice: How the Hyde Amendment Harms Poor Women" (New York: Center for Reproductive Rights, 2010).

Edin, Kathryn and Maria Kefelas. *Promises I Can Keep: Why Poor Women Put Motherhood before Marriage* (Berkeley: University of California Press, 2005).

Fetal Bodies and Reproductive Politics

Dubow, Sarah. *Ourselves Unborn: A History of the Fetus in Modern America* (New York: Oxford University Press, 2010).

Roth, Rachel. *Making Women Pay: The Hidden Costs of Fetal Rights* (Ithaca, NY: Cornell University Press, 2003).

Reproductive Technologies

Glover, Jonathan. *Choosing Children: Genes, Disability, and Design* (New York: Oxford University Press, 2008).

Hvistendahl, Mara. *Unnatural Selection: Choosing Boys over Girls, and the Consequences of a World Full of Men* (New York: Public Affairs, 2011).

Ikemoto, Lisa C. "Eggs as Capital: Human Egg Procurement in the Fertility Industry and the Stem Cell Research Enterprise," *Signs* 34 (Summer 2009): 763–782

Roberts, Dorothy E. "Race, Gender, and Genetic Technologies: A New Reproductive Dystopia?" *Signs* 34 (Summer 2009): 783–804.

Sandel, Michael. *The Case against Perfection: Ethics in the Age of Genetic Engineering* (Cambridge, MA: Harvard University Press, 2009).

Spar, Deborah L., *The Baby Business: How Money, Science, and Politics Drive the Commerce of Conception* (Boston: Harvard Business School Press, 2006).

Adoption and Foster Care

Briggs, Laura. *Somebody's Children* (Durham, NC: Duke University Press, 2012).

Dorow, Sara. Transnational Adoption: A Cultural Economy of Race, Gender, and Kinship (New York: New York University Press, 2006).

Goodwin, Michele Bratcher, ed. *Baby Markets: Money and the New Politics of Creating Families* (Cambridge: Cambridge University Press, 2008).

Johnson, Kay. *Wanting a Daughter, Needing a Son: Abandonment, Adoption, and Orphanage Care in China* (St. Paul, MN; Yeong and Yeong, 2004).

Kim, Elena J. *Adopted Territory: Transnational Korean Adoptees and the Politics of Belonging* (Durham, NC: Duke University Press, 2010).

Roberts, Dorothy. *Shattered Bonds: The Color of Child Welfare* (New York: Basic Books, 2002).

Solinger, Rickie. *Beggars and Choosers: How the Politics of Choice Shapes Adoption, Abortion, and Welfare in the United States* (New York: Hill and Wang, 2002).

The Environment and Reproduction

Schettler, Ted, Gina Solomon, Maria Valenti, and Annette Huddle. *Generations at Risk: Reproductive Health and the Environment* (Cambridge, MA: MIT Press, 1999.)

"Shaping Our Legacy: Reproductive Health and the Environment," Program of Reproductive Health and the Environment (San Francisco: University of California-San Francisco, 2007).

Boswell-Penc, Mia. Tainted Milk: *Breastmilk, Feminism, and the Politics of Environmental Degradation* (Albany, NY: State University of New York Press, 2006).

Woodruff, Tracey J., Sarah J. Janssen, Louis J. Guillette, Jr., and Linda C. Giudice, eds. *Environmental Impacts on Reproductive Health and Fertility* (Cambridge: Cambridge University Press, 2010).

Incarcerated Women and Reproductive Politics

Golden, Renny. *War on the Family: Mothers in Prison and the Families They Leave Behind* (New York: Routledge, 2005).

Law Students for Reproductive Justice. "Reproductive Justice in the Prison System," Law Students for Reproductive Justice pamphlet, 2010.

Roth, Rachel. "Searching for the State: Who Governs Prisoners' Reproductive Rights?" Social Politics 11(Fall 2004): 411–438.

Solinger, Rickie, Paula Johnson, Martha Raimon, Tina Reynolds, and Ruby Tapia, eds. *Interrupted Life: Experiences of Incarcerated Women in the U.S.* (Berkeley: University of California Press, 2010).

Reproductive Health

Boston Women's Health Book Collective. *Our Bodies, Ourselves: Pregnancy and Birth* (New York: Simon & Schuster, 2008).

Kline, Wendy. *Bodies of Knowledge: Sexuality, Reproduction, and Women's Health in the Second Wave* (Chicago: University of Chicago Press, 2010).

Movahed, Michelle, and Cindy Soohoo. "Report on the United States' Compliance with Its Human Rights Obligations in the Area of Women's Reproductive and Sexual Health" (New York: Center for Reproductive Rights, 2010).

Sills, Sarah R., Robert Jaffe, and Lourdes A. Rivera. *Protecting Reproductive Health Care for Low Income Women* (New York: NYS-NARAL Foundation, 2002).

Sex Education

Dailard, Cynthia. Understanding "Abstinence": Implications for Individuals, Programs and Policies" Guttmacher Report on Public Policy (New York: Guttmacher Institute, December 2003).

Fields, Jessica. *Risky Lessons: Sex Education and Social Inequality* (New Brunswick, NJ: Rutgers University Press, 2008).

Irvine, Janice. *Talk about Sex: The Battles over Sex Education in the United States* (Berkeley: University of California Press, 2004).

Disability and Reproduction

Generations Ahead. Bridging the Divide: Disability Rights and Justice Advocates Discussing Genetic Technologies (Oakland, CA: Generations Ahead, 2007–2008).

Parens, Eric, and Adrienne Asch. *Prenatal Testing and Disability Rights* (Washington, DC: GeorgetownUniversity Press, 2000).

Reagan, Leslie J. *Dangerous Pregnancies Mothers, Disabilities, and Abortion in Modern America* (Berkeley: University of California Press, 2010).

Tremain, Shelley. "Reproductive Freedom, Self-Regulation, and the Government of Impairment in Utero." *Hypatia* 21 (Winter 2006): 35–53.

LGBTQI Family-Building

Agigian, Amy. *Baby Steps: How Lesbian Alternative Insemination Is Changing the World* (Middletown, CT: Wesleyan, 2004).

Lewin, Ellen. *Gay Fatherhood: Narratives of Family and Citizenship in America* (Chicago: University of Chicago Press, 2009).

Luce, Jacquelyne. *Beyond Expectation: Lesbian/Bi/Queer Women and Assisted Conception* (Toronto: University of Toronto Press, 2010).

Mamo, Laura. *Queering Reproduction: Achieving Pregnancy in the Age of Technoscience* (Durham, NC: Duke University Press, 2007).

Weston, Kath. *Families We Choose: Lesbians, Gays, Kinship* (New York: Columbia University Press; rev. ed., 1997).

Birthing in the United States

Block, Jennifer. *Pushed: The Painful Truth about Childbirth and Modern Maternity Care* (New York: De Capo Press. 2007).

Leavitt, Judith Waltzer. *Brought to Bed: Childbearing in America, 1750–1950* (New York: Oxford University Press, 1986).

Wagner, Marsden. *Born in the USA: How a Broken Maternity System Must Be Fixed to Put Women and Children First* (Berkeley: University of California Press, 2008).

Reproductive Justice

Silliman, Jael, Marlene Gerber Fried, Loretta Ross, and Elena R. Gutiérrez, eds., *Undivided Rights: Women of Color Organize for Reproductive Justice* (Boston: South End Press, 2004).

Solinger, Rickie. "The First Welfare Case: Money, Sex, Marriage and White Supremacy in Selma, 1966—A Reproductive Justice Analysis," *Journal of Women's History* 22 (Fall 2010): 13–38.

INDEX

private insurance to cover
    abortion, 85
privilege
    adoption, racial superiority and
        privilege, 118
    class privilege, assisted
        reproductive technologies
        (ART), 111
Pro-Life Legal Affairs Committee
    created by National
    Conference of Catholic
    Bishops, 16
Protestant denominations
    abortion, 35, 39
    Comstock, Anthony, 35
    contraception, 35
    dissemination of information,
        criminalized, 35
    fetus, establishment of
        personhood or ensoulment,
        34
    moral reformers, public
        opposition to
        contraception, 35
public education forums, pre-*Roe
    v. Wade*, 25
public hearings, feminism, 25
public policy, 45–49
    Aid to Dependent Children
        (ADC) program, 47
    Aid to Families with Dependent
        Children (AFDC), 47–48
    child-protective services, 48–49
        poor parents, cultural
        misunderstandings and
        bias-driven problems, 49
    day-care funding, 45, 46
    drug policies, 46–47
    family leave, 45, 46
    foster care option, 48–49

gender-based wage disparities,
    46
    Latina women, gender-based
        wage disparities, 46
    paid parental leave, 45
    public *vs.* private debate of sex
        and reproduction, 2–3
    Temporary Assistance to Needy
        Families (TANF), 48
    welfare policy, 47–48
public *vs.* private debate of sex
    and reproduction, 2–3

Qatar, abortion, 38
queer. *See* LGBTQI persons
        (lesbian, gay, bi-sexual,
        transgender, queer, intersex
        persons)
quickening, 4, 5
Quran, stages of embryonic
        development, 37

race and class bias, men, 142
race matching, adoption, 117
racial superiority and privilege,
    adoption, 118
racism, eugenic laws, 8
Reagan, Ronald
    abortion, 17
    fetal pain, evidence, 94
    Helms Amendment, 146
    United Nations Population
        Fund (UNFPA), 148
    welfare policy, 47
Reform Judaism, 39
religion, 34–40
    Catholic Church, contraception
        and abortion, 34, 36–37, 39
    Christianity, abortion and
        contraception, 34